DATING the DIVORCED MAN

CHRISTIE HARTMAN, PH.D.

Sort Through the Baggage to
Decide if He's Right for You

AVON, MASSACHUSETTS

Published by
Adams Media, an F+W Publications Company
57 Littlefield Street, Avon, MA 02322 U.S.A.
www.adamsmedia.com

ISBN 10: 1-59869-141-4
ISBN 13: 978-1-59869-141-2

Printed in the United States of America.

J I H G F E D C B

Library of Congress Cataloging-in-Publication Data
is available from publisher.

This publication is designed to provide accurate and authoritative
information with regard to the subject matter covered. It is sold with
the understanding that the publisher is not engaged in rendering legal,
accounting, or other professional advice. If legal advice or other expert
assistance is required, the services of a competent professional person
should be sought.

—From a *Declaration of Principles* jointly adopted by a
Committee of the American Bar Association and
a Committee of Publishers and Associations

Many of the designations used by manufacturers and sellers to distin-
guish their product are claimed as trademarks. Where those designations appear in this book and Adams Media was aware of a trademark
claim, the designations have been printed with initial capital letters.

This book is available at quantity discounts for bulk purchases.
For information, please call 1-800-289-0963.

This book is dedicated to my mom,
who has always encouraged me.

Contents

Acknowledgments

I want to thank the following people, who helped make this book happen and who supported me during the creation of it: my family, including Steve, Jon Mark, and Joshua, my mom and Morris, my dad and Suzanne, and Leslee; my friends Lana, Marti, Shannon, Lizzie, Lisa, Martin, and Julie.

I also want to acknowledge all the men and women who provided the stories and examples I presented in this book. Thank you for sharing your lives and insights with me.

Introduction

Recently, while browsing online, I found an article in which a woman asked a dating expert for advice. This woman had met a divorced man, but felt concerned because he had a young child and an ex-wife—in other words, he had baggage. Not accustomed to dating divorced men with children, she wanted to know what she was getting into. The expert scoffed at this woman's reticence—sure, the expert said, divorced men have ex-wives, children, and lots of other baggage. But pick your poison, she continued, because never-married men have problems of their own, including a lack of desire to commit or mixed messages about what they want. At least a divorced man can commit, the expert said. I shook my head at what I read, because this "expert" missed the whole point. This woman wanted some advice to prepare her for what to expect, and was told that the realities of a divorced man with a child were no more difficult than those of a never-married man. I *completely* disagree. Besides, being divorced and laden with baggage does *not* render a man immune to commitment-phobia or mixed messages.

The truth is, separated and divorced men differ from men who have not been married before. How are they different, you ask? Although every separated or divorced man varies in his circumstances, these men typically have more challenges than never-married men. For starters, these men have a marriage under their belts—and marriages have complexities not seen in most nonmarital relationships. They have ex-wives—and these women can be considerably more influential than an ex-girlfriend. They may also have children, child support and maintenance payments, residual emotional issues, and a host of other challenges. For the single woman, this can be a lot to take on! In this book, I will discuss all the different types of challenges that come with separated and divorced men, and show you how to handle them. You will learn to:

- Detect problems early on—and tackle them.
- Quickly weed out men who will be bad partners.
- Recognize a good partner and create a successful partnership with him.
- Identify problems that "come with the territory" versus those that are unacceptable.
- Evaluate whether marriage to a divorced man is the right choice for you.

You'll also learn to ask the important questions, such as:

- When is a divorced man ready to date?
- How do you spot a man on the rebound?
- Do his children come first?
- Is it okay for him to spend time with his ex?

Before you dig in, however, there are a few other important things you should know:

This book does not advocate settling. Settling is accepting less than what you really want and need in a relationship. Settling is the enemy of successful relationships, whether with a divorced man or any man. I will provide tools to help you find a relationship that makes you happy and fulfilled.

This book will not judge you. Despite my high standards for you, I support any decision you make—only *you* know what's best for you. My goal is to give you as much information as possible, and then you can make your own informed decision.

This book emphasizes problem-solving. One thing I've noticed about some dating and relationship books is that they spend too much time storytelling and not enough time teaching important principles and giving straight-up advice. Stories are important, and I include many stories in this book, but I emphasize identifying problems and fixing them.

This book will not teach you how to "win" him. I will not show you how to catch a divorced man, win over his children, or make his ex-wife happy. I also won't focus on methods to help him get over his divorce, help him deal with his ex, or otherwise show you how to be a good girlfriend. Why? Because you shouldn't try to win him—*he* should try to win *you*. This book focuses on getting *your* needs met, and will help you evaluate whether your relationship with him can do that.

This book defines success by happiness, not togetherness. Anyone can tell you how to catch a man. And anyone can tell you how to tenaciously trudge through a difficult relationship. But I want to aim for something more for you: I want you to be *happy* with your man. If you aren't happy, what's the point? Thus, my goal isn't to help you make your relationship with your separated or divorced man work no matter what, it's to make sure you're happy, even if that means leaving the relationship.

Overall, this book will provide you with plenty of information and advice for dating separated and divorced men. Yes, these men can come with challenges, but you will learn how to identify and handle these challenges like a pro. Then you can achieve the happy, healthy relationship you want!

The World of Separated and Divorced Men

As a psychologist, I have observed, researched, and interviewed numerous separated and divorced men, and the women who date them. And as a woman, I have dated a few of them myself! Because of these experiences, I made several discoveries, such as:

Separated and divorced men are everywhere. In today's world, nearly every woman will date a separated or divorced man sometime during her single life. With more than 50 percent of marriages ending in divorce, men who were previously unavailable have re-entered the dating pool and now make up nearly 40 percent of available men. In addition, women are waiting longer than ever before to get married, and this increases their chances of meeting a man who has already been married.

Separated and divorced men are dating. Divorce and relationship books have cited research concluding that men, much more than women, are less likely to waste time getting back in the dating game after they become separated. When dealing with the loss of a marriage, men are more likely to take action and move on with someone new, whereas women tend to talk about their loss and not rush into something new. In addition, men with children have more time to date than do women with children because they typically get less parenting time after divorce. However, this has changed more recently as our legal system has begun to recognize fathers' rights.

Separated and divorced men remarry. According to Sam Margulies, Ph.D., J.D., author of *A Man's Guide to a Civilized Divorce: How to Divorce with Grace, a Little Class, and a Lot of Common Sense,* not only do most divorced men (more than 75 percent) remarry, they typically do so within a few years of their divorces. Divorced women move at a slower pace, and take longer to remarry. However, second marriages fail at an even higher rate than first marriages, so it's important to have guidance while dating a divorced man.

Separated and divorced men come with challenges. Sure, no man is perfect. However, separated and divorced men differ from their never-married counterparts in some key ways—they often come with challenges that go above and beyond what you will find with the average man. Moreover, many women have never encountered most of these challenges before, and may not know how to handle children, difficult ex-wives, reticent parents, substantial financial obligations to the ex, or his anger, guilt, or unresolved grief. Without sufficient information and guidance, women who date these men often experience difficulties or become unhappy.

Women often don't mind a man with children. Some divorced men have children. Other men have children even though they've never been married. Typically, women are more willing than men to date someone with children. Some time ago, I was eating dinner with my partner at a local restaurant. A man and a woman, both in their thirties, sat at the table next to us. I could overhear some of their conversation, and it didn't take long to figure out that they were on their first date. They began to discuss more personal things, and he revealed that he had three children. He seemed a little sheepish, as she had no children and had never even been married. Her response to his three children was "That's cool!" In other words, she seemed totally open to his situation.

Many women are unprepared for the problems that come with these men. Despite the increasing number of separated and divorced men, until now there was very little support and guidance for the women who date these men. If you perused the relationship section of any large bookstore, you would have found many books on relationships and dating, but nothing on dating separated and divorced men. You would also have found books on marriage, including stepparenting, stepmothering, and being a "second wife"—yet nearly every problem faced by women married to divorced men actually begins *during the dating process.* The sooner these problems are identified, the greater chance of solving them. Too often, women wind up in bad relationships or marriages with divorced men because they had no guidance on how to spot trouble ahead of time.

In addition, the women who date these men are often given vague or mixed messages. Here's an example: a dating expert will tell you that when you date a divorced man with children, his children will always come first. You will hear this mantra a dozen times, but these experts never tell you what it means.

Does "his children come first" mean:

- Children have needs that their parents must fulfill?
- Children's needs are much more important than adult needs?
- Children require lots of time, money, and patience?
- He can't blow off his child's soccer game in order to have brunch with you?
- He will never love you as much as he loves his children?

These are very different questions. "The children come first" can mean different things to different people—thus, I will discuss this important concept in this book.

Many women struggle as stepmothers and "second wives." I have observed some painful situations with women who marry divorced men and wind up feeling stressed, misunderstood, ignored, disrespected, or left out. Of course, not all stepmothers and second wives experience these things, but the ones who do suffer. Again, if they'd had guidance before they married, perhaps they could have prevented some of the problems they're dealing with now.

Here are two stories that illustrate the challenges that a separated or divorced man can bring to the relationship:

ꙮ Donna met Peter through a mutual acquaintance. Peter was divorced and had three school-age children. They began dating, their relationship got serious, and Donna eventually moved in with Peter. Then something unexpected happened: Peter's ex-wife was injured in a serious car accident that took her nearly a year to recover from. Donna became a surrogate mother—she took care of Peter's children while he was working. When Peter needed to move for the children's sake, Donna quit her job and took a lesser job in order to be with him. After three years, Peter gave Donna a ring and talked about getting married. Then Peter changed his mind—he broke up with Donna, told her he didn't love her anymore, and asked her to move out of his home. The children were heartbroken. And Donna was left with nothing— she'd given it all up to be with Peter.

When Penelope met Jason, they hit it off immediately. They began dating, and developed strong feelings for one another. However, Jason had one flaw: he was still getting divorced. But Jason told Penelope that his divorce would only take three months, and Penelope believed that things would work out for them. Jason's divorce ended up taking a year. During that year, Penelope was exposed to the hatred of Jason's ex-wife, the disapproval of his parents, and the dirty details of Jason's extremely acrimonious divorce. Nobody she knew had ever been through anything like this, so Penelope had to figure things out on her own. At one point, at her wits' end, Penelope said to her best friend, "How did this happen? I can't take this anymore."

If these sound like horror stories to you, you're right— they are. And, like all the stories in this book, they are true. Both Donna and Penelope met, dated, and fell in love with a separated or divorced man. Neither woman had any idea of what she was getting into. Both were overwhelmed by unfamiliar and unexpected challenges, creating unhappiness and struggle in their lives. Donna and Penelope aren't alone— many women have struggled with the unfamiliar challenges that come with these men. And that is why I wrote this book. If you want to learn how to prevent painful situations like these, read on!

ONE

What's So Special about
Separated and Divorced Men?

Katie, a good friend of mine, travels a lot because of her job. She is outgoing and tends to meet people wherever she goes. On a business trip to a small town, she met a local man while eating in a restaurant. They had lunch together. He was getting divorced, but the divorce was proceeding smoothly. At his invitation, she had dinner at his house a couple of nights later. Since his town was small, she walked to his house. They enjoyed a nice dinner, and before he could get any ideas, Katie stood up to say goodnight. As she was leaving, he asked if he could drive her, as he didn't want his neighbors to see a woman coming out of his house at night. It would look bad for the divorce, he said. She agreed. Once in his car, he asked her if she would duck down and hide, so nobody would see her in his car as he drove. Katie, unprepared for these requests and trying to be understanding, agreed again. He drove her back to her hotel.

Katie's seemingly simple dinner with a nice man turned into a complicated situation, where she was put in a difficult position. That's the tricky thing with separated and divorced men—they often appear simpler than they are, and they pose unexpected challenges to the women who get involved.

What Makes Separated and Divorced Men Different?

So what is it that makes separated and divorced men different? Unless you are very young, any man you date will have had past relationships, right? Some men will have emotional baggage from those relationships, right? This section will touch upon several ways separated and divorced men are different from never-married men.

They've Had a "Failed" Marriage

When two people create a relationship together, they may hope that the relationship will work out over the long haul. When two people marry one another, it is their very *intention* for things to work out over the long haul. Nobody marries with the intention of getting divorced. Thus, for many men, the end of a marriage can generate a greater feeling of failure than that resulting from the end of nonmarital relationships. These men get a new demographic label—instead of being single or married, they're "divorced." For some men, this label alone may conjure up feelings of failure and render them more hesitant to make another commitment.

They Have Children

Many marriages result in children. But unlike marital commitments, which can end at any time, a commitment to a child is forever. Children require considerable amounts of attention, care, time, and money, and dating a man with children is nothing like dating a man without them. Children also generate a permanent connection with an ex-wife, the mother of his children. And through her, the children will always have a second set of relatives—grandparents, cousins, aunts, uncles, etc.—who may or may not welcome you. Of course, some men have children but have never been married—this book applies to these men as well.

They Have Ex-wives

Although any guy can have an ex-girlfriend, separated and divorced men have ex-wives. For some men, there is little difference between the two. However, for other men, an ex-wife may have a stronger pull on his emotions than an ex-girlfriend. He may remain friends with her after they divorce, or perhaps he pays her a sum of money each month. And if they had children together, the ex plays a permanent role in his life. Also, along with this ex-wife come additional family ties. Marriage creates new family bonds—in-laws. Divorce severs these bonds legally, but not necessarily emotionally. Thus, his family may have a relationship with his ex, and he may have relationships with his ex and her family. If there are children, the ties to his ex and her family are permanent—his children are their "blood."

They Have Monthly Payments

Most adults make monthly payments to have the things they want or need, including car payments, house payments, and credit card payments. However, divorced men can have two types of payments that are unique to them: child support payments and spousal maintenance payments (i.e., alimony). Not only do these payments cut into the divorced man's income, but they represent a link to his former marriage. In the case of alimony, he's making monthly payments not for something he owns, but to someone who is no longer in his day-to-day life. Thus, the divorced man may be financially strapped and not able to court you the way he'd like to.

They May Still Be Married

A significant portion of this book is devoted to men who are separated or going through a divorce. This is a unique situation—from a relationship standpoint these men are single, but from a legal standpoint they are still married. This introduces a series of challenges and problems that you would never see with other men.

The differences between separated/divorced men and never-married men are apparent. But how do these differences translate into difficulties?

What Makes These Relationships Difficult?

Relationships with separated and divorced men can come with many challenges, some of which include children, ex-wives, financial problems, and emotional wounds. I will discuss these challenges, and many more, in detail throughout this book. However, there are several less obvious (but just as challenging) factors that make relationships with separated and divorced men difficult, such as the following:

Unrealistic Expectations

Without realizing it, most of us base our expectations about our relationships on what we experienced in previous relationships. Or, we base our expectations on what we see depicted in movies and on TV. Unfortunately, TV, movies, and relationships with men who've never been married won't adequately prepare you for the challenges of dating separated and divorced men. For example, many movies depicting the life of a single parent often portray the child as unusually mature (often more so than the parent), and extremely open to the parent's new partner. The child's other parent is usually out of the picture, or very understanding. Things don't usually work this way in the real world.

Lack of Information

The difficulty of these relationships also stems from a lack of available information about them. How do you recognize signs of trouble? How do you handle problems that arise? What are the standards for what is acceptable and what is not? There are few resources that adequately address these relationships. To further confuse the issue, the information that does exist gives women vague or mixed messages on important issues. For example, these resources may tell you to accept the divorced man's relationship with his ex, especially if they have children together. But such a relationship can vary from businesslike to chummy, and these resources don't elaborate on what is and is not appropriate behavior with an ex.

Unmet Needs

Because relationships with separated and divorced men can come with unfamiliar challenges, there is greater risk that the women who date these men may not get their needs met. The reason for this is twofold: (1) it's difficult to know what you'll need in a situation you've never been in and (2) your needs may get overshadowed by the needs of his children, his ex, his family, etc. Moreover, inexperience makes it difficult to recognize that this is happening! For example, you are dating a man with children, and he routinely interrupts or cancels dates because his children or ex-wife have some sort of crisis. How do you handle this situation?

Unclear Boundaries

When you date a separated or divorced man, in some ways you wind up "dating" his children, his ex-wife, and a myriad of other family members. Why? The bonds he formed during his marriage aren't easily severed. This is especially true if he has children, as they create a permanent link to his past. These bonds and links, if not properly managed, can create a host of boundary issues for him, his children, his ex, his family, and you. I have a saying that I will use many times throughout this book: **unclear boundaries equal trouble.** For example, a divorced man frequently gives his ex-wife money or helps her fix her car. Is this appropriate, or a sign of improper boundaries?

Lack of Support

When you get involved with a separated or divorced man and encounter unfamiliar challenges, whom do you consult for support? Hopefully you have friends, a therapist, or other people to provide support during tough times. However, unless you know someone who has experience with these men, you may feel all alone. And unfortunately, there are few books that provide support in this area. Thus, an important reason I wrote this book was not only to provide information, but also to provide support.

Clearly, there are numerous factors that make relationships with separated and divorced men challenging for women.

However, this does not mean that these men are trouble, or that you should avoid relationships with these men—like most things in life, separated and divorced men have their pros and cons.

Pros and Cons of Separated and Divorced Men

As explained earlier in this chapter, separated and divorced men are different in some key ways, and they have their own set of pros and cons. Your goal, throughout this book and over time, is to determine which pros are most important to you, and which cons are the "deal-breakers." Following are just some of the pros and cons of dating separated and divorced men.

The Pros

While these benefits will not apply to every case, here are some of the main pros that may come along with dating a separated or divorced man.

HE'S AVAILABLE
Once a man breaks off his marital relationship and moves into a place of his own, he is technically available to date, even if his divorce hasn't ended (or even really begun). This is one good aspect of divorce—it can make available those men who would otherwise have been off limits forever, maybe even "the one who got away."

HE'S APPRECIATIVE
Once the grief has worn off, it isn't uncommon for a separated or divorced man to really appreciate a good woman, as he probably spent years squabbling with a woman who

was wrong for him. If he has learned from his mistakes, he will appreciate the next woman he chooses to spend his time with.

HE'S EXPERIENCED

This man has been around the block. He knows something about what's involved in making a marriage work, even if his ultimately didn't. Some people may assume that divorce is an indication of an inability to make a relationship work, not realizing that all those years before a divorce occurs are spent trying to make things work, teaching the couple valuable lessons about relationships. Many of these men are looking for another chance to "get it right." If he has children, that's even more valuable experience. He's more experienced at dealing with women and handling conflict, and he probably won't wig out if you have a meltdown one day. He should also be used to paying attention to a woman's needs in the bedroom. Overall, experience usually makes for a better relationship, as he can learn from his past mistakes.

HE'S MATURE

Maturity is a nice side effect of experience. Marriage and divorce don't guarantee maturity, but the responsibilities of marriage and especially children often go a long way toward increasing maturity levels in men. A divorced man probably has an edge over his never-married buddies in terms of how to handle women, children, finances, and other aspects of everyday life. And he's less likely to be out getting drunk with the guys every night.

HE CAN COMMIT

For all you women who have banged your heads against the wall dealing with commitment-phobes, the separated or divorced man has proven that he is interested in making a long-term commitment, even if his first attempt did not work out in the long run. Although some separated and divorced men may shy away from commitment, they probably won't do so for long: the vast majority (more than 75 percent) of divorced men remarry, and they generally do so within a few years of their divorces.

The Cons

And of course, there are some cons that may come up in your relationship with a separated or divorced man.

HE'S HURT

A divorce can leave a tough legacy, not only financially but emotionally. To grieve the loss of his marriage is perfectly natural—in fact, it's totally necessary. But men vary greatly in how they grieve, and in how long it takes them to grieve. It isn't uncommon for a separated or divorced man to start up with another woman before the grief process has completed, which creates problems for the woman. In addition, he may show some defensiveness with you if you do something that reminds him of his ex—for example, if his ex cheated on him, he may overreact to your having lunch with a male friend.

HE HAS KIDS

Many divorced men have children. Of course, kids themselves are not bad. However, they have a huge impact on his life, and dating a man with kids who belong to someone else can have lots of challenges. For example, kids mean the continual involvement of his ex-wife in his life, which can create problems. Kids need a lot of care and attention, which, depending on the situation, can put some limitations on such choices as how you spend your spare time or where you live. Kids are perhaps the most important reason you should be circumspect in dating a divorced man.

HE HAS AN EX-WIFE

Like children, an ex is not a bad thing in and of itself, and an ex-wife is not necessarily an evil woman whom you should fear or avoid. After all, most grown men have ex-girlfriends. But with separated and divorced men, an ex-wife may hover in the shadows. And some ex-wives can cause a lot of problems, especially if she isn't over him, he isn't over her, they have children together, or he is still partially responsible for her financial well-being.

HE'S POOR

Divorce is expensive, in terms of both direct divorce costs and the resulting fallout when the divorce ends. Often, divorce leaves men with less stuff (money, home, and belongings) and more bills (debts, child support, and alimony).

HE'S NOT READY FOR A RELATIONSHIP

Sometimes men emerge from a marriage with a case of commitment-phobia. Some men avoid dating for a while or, more commonly, they keep their relationships at a casual level. These men commonly engage in rebound relationships.

Now that I've discussed some of the basics that make separated and divorced men special, it's time to explain some of the more fundamental concepts of dating these men: The five principles of dating separated and divorced men, and Input versus Output. I will refer to these concepts throughout this book, as they are important in evaluating your relationship with him.

Not All Separated and Divorced Men Are Created Equal

As you read this book, you will come across a plethora of potential problems and issues that can come up when dating separated and divorced men. However, every separated or divorced man is unique, and each will have different problems. Some of these men have very little baggage and aren't that different from men who've never been married. Others are so baggage-laden that getting involved with them is a nightmare. Most fall somewhere in between. Before I present you with all the possible ex-wife, children, family, and money issues that these men can come with, here are the five fundamental principles that predict how difficult a relationship with this man will be:

THE FIVE PRINCIPLES THAT INFLUENCE THE DIFFICULTY OF YOUR RELATIONSHIP

1. His marital status
2. The length of time since his divorce finalized
3. The length of his marriage
4. The reason for the divorce
5. Children

Let's take a closer look at these principles.

Principle 1: His Marital Status

This book discusses two basic categories of men who've been married before: separating men and divorced men.

Separating men. These men live separately from their spouses, but their divorces have not finalized yet. Because

separating men have several unique challenges that warrant extra discussion, I further divide this group into two
sub-categories:

- Separated men: These men haven't filed for divorce
  yet, or they have but are not really proceeding with it.
- Divorcing men: These men have filed for divorce and
  are in the process of divorcing.

Divorced men. These men are legally and officially
divorced.

A marriage comprises two components: the relationship
bond and the legal bond. Divorced men have severed their
legal bond to their ex, and most have ended the relationship
bond as well. On the other hand, separated and divorcing
men still retain the legal bond to their ex, which creates several complications. These men may still retain some element
of the relationship bond with their exes as well. The closer
he is to legal divorce, the greater the chance he will be ready
to move on. The bottom line: separated and divorcing men
come with more difficulties than divorced men, and separated men have the most potential for problems.

Principle 2: The Length of Time since His Divorce Finalized

It's no surprise that a recently divorced man will have
more issues than one who's been divorced for years. A newly
divorced man may still be grieving, as may his children, his
ex, and his family. Everybody must adjust to new custody
arrangements, new financial arrangements, and new living
arrangements. By contrast, a long-divorced man is more
likely to have worked all this out and created a life he is
comfortable with. He's had more time to move on and get

financially stable, his children and ex are used to divorced life, or his children have already grown up.

Principle 3: The Length of His Marriage

Divorcing after a long marriage usually predicts greater emotional entwinement, and therefore a longer grieving period for everybody involved, including children, the ex, and the extended family. A longer marriage means a much greater likelihood of children, and greater financial fallout with divorce. It greatly increases the chances of his having to pay alimony, and the longer they were married, the longer he has to pay. Shorter marriages tend to end with fewer problems and have fewer attachments; exes tend to feel less "ownership" and old habits haven't become permanently ingrained.

Principle 4: The Reason for the Divorce

There are many reasons why people divorce, but for your purposes, some are better than others. If he wanted the divorce, chances are he is more ready to move on with his life and to begin a relationship with someone new. However, his children, family, and especially his ex won't be so ready, and will take longer than he does to accept the changes. If she wanted the divorce, she is less likely to be jealous of you or otherwise difficult with him, especially if she moves on with another man. However, if he didn't want the divorce, he may not have much to offer for a while. The best-case scenario is if they both wanted the divorce—but this rarely happens. Moreover, if they divorced because of incompatibility or "irreconcilable differences," he is more likely to move on and find a better relationship. Marriages that involved infidelity, abuse, or other serious problems tend to leave more emotional baggage.

Principle 5: Children

Children take divorce, and the period after divorce, to a whole new level. Not only are children a huge commitment by themselves, but with them comes an ex-wife, lots of family members, financial commitments, and conflicts over what's best for them. Kids are the most important factor in predicting how difficult things will be for you when you date a separated or divorced man.

The Difficulty Index

Once you examine the above five principles, you can summarize them by using the Difficulty Index. The Difficulty Index is a quick reference to how challenging a relationship with him will be, all other factors being equal. The table below divides separated and divorced men into three categories based on the above five principles:

HIGH DIFFICULTY INDEX

- All men with children
- All separated men
- Divorcing men with no children, divorce was initiated by her

MEDIUM DIFFICULTY INDEX

- Divorcing men with no children, divorce was initiated by him
- Recently divorced men with no children, divorce initiated by her
- Divorced men with no children, long marriage

LOW DIFFICULTY INDEX

- Men divorced for many years, no children
- Divorced men with no children, short marriage
- Men with no children, mutual agreement to divorce

The higher the Difficulty Index, the more complicated the issues, the more difficult the relationship, and the more caution you should take.

One last thing: the Difficulty Index is an indicator, not a guarantee. Every man is different—thus, use the Difficulty Index only as a guideline when dating these men.

Evaluating Your Relationship:
Input Versus Output

When you date a separated or divorced man, he may come with many different types of challenges. Over time, these challenges can prove to be "worth it," or they can prove to be not worth the effort. Therefore, you will need a tool to evaluate your relationship. You can do this by examining Input versus Output: in other words, how much you're putting into the relationship (Input) versus how much you're getting out of the relationship (Output). How do you define Input and Output?

Input

Input is affected by the number and complexity of challenges that your divorced man brings to the table, including children, an ex-wife, difficult family or friends, money problems, and any divorce-related emotional baggage. The more baggage he has, and the more difficulties there are, the greater your Input. Input also includes how much you have to compromise your way of life to accommodate a man, his kids, his ex, his family, and his finances. For example, have all your weekends, which used to be spent having dinner and drinks with friends, turned into changing diapers and trips to amusement parks? A changed life doesn't have to mean a compromised one—only you can tell the difference. Your level of Input is something you will evaluate as you read through this book.

Output

Output is measured by all the good things you get from your relationship, including love, support, good sex, gifts, fun times, good conversation, and companionship. In other words, Output includes all those things you want and need in a relationship.

In order to have a satisfying relationship, your Output must exceed your Input. How do you know when this happens? No relationship is perfect, and all relationships have occasional conflicts—but when your Output is high enough relative to your Input, you will feel satisfied with your relationship the vast majority of the time. The cool thing about Input versus Output is that it's customized to each woman— what's difficult for you may be easy for another woman, and what makes you happy may not be enough for another woman. Overall, if you take anything from this book, take this: learn to evaluate your Input versus your Output. The greater your Output relative to your Input, the happier you will be.

The reverse is also true: when your Output isn't enough to compensate for your Input, I refer to that as a "Low Output" situation. A Low Output situation will take a toll on your happiness over time. A common Low Output situation that I've seen with women is when they become "rescuers." In these situations, a woman gets involved with a divorced man with kids, encounters a myriad of problems (such as troublesome children, difficult exes, or debts), and then seeks to solve those problems in order to create a healthier situation for all. She will try to care for his children, handle his difficult ex, and fill in his financial holes with her own money. The problem is, there's only so much she can do to fix these problems—they aren't really her problems at all, but they've been heaped on her because of her relationship. She doesn't get enough in return (Output) for her efforts (Input), and this imbalance inevitably leads to her unhappiness.

Thus, no matter how simple or difficult his situation is, what you need to examine most is how happy and satisfied you are. Anybody can scratch and struggle their way through a relationship and keep it together, but not everybody who does so achieves satisfaction. Remember: the goal is to be happy.

TWO

Proceed with Caution:
The Soon-to-Be-Separated Man

A soon-to-be-separated man still resides with his spouse, but entertains the idea of leaving her. You may wonder why a section on these men is included in this book. It's not because dating a soon-to-be-separated man is a good idea; rather, it's because there is a point before the filing of divorce papers when a man will start wondering about other women. For some men, wondering can lead to involvement. It is also the point at which a man will begin to look single, attracting the interest of women.

The following paragraphs are two examples of such a circumstance.

🐾 Charlene worked with Jim for four years. They got along well, but Charlene never considered anything beyond a platonic relationship because Jim was married. One day, Jim told Charlene that he and his wife were considering divorce. Soon he began looking for a place to live. Charlene began to feel attracted to Jim, and was very surprised when Jim began to show interest in her.

 When Maria met Jay through mutual friends, she didn't realize Jay was married until someone mentioned it, as he behaved like a single man. It turns out he'd been planning to divorce his wife for months, but was too financially constrained to move out of their home. He began talking to Maria, then calling her, and expressed interest in knowing her better.

Clearly, both Jim and Jay are married men. However, these men have crossed that invisible line, where the seeds of divorce have begun to sprout—they find themselves interested in women, and women find themselves interested in them. Thus, the reason you should know more about dating soon-to-be-separated men is because, for some men, dating can begin here. Soon-to-be-separated men fall into three categories:

Men Who Will Never Leave Their Marriages: These men complain about their marriages and their wives, but don't have the "stones" to leave the marriage. They talk as if they will, but they always find an excuse why they can't. These men often wind up turning to other women, via extramarital affairs, for solace and validation.

Men Who Will Eventually Leave Their Marriages but Aren't Ready to Yet: These men typically know their marriages are over, but haven't fully accepted it yet. They still hope things will work out, or they fear venturing into the unknown. They often have plenty of excuses for why they can't leave. These men may look to a new woman as an excuse to leave the marriage.

Men Who Are in the Process of Leaving Their Marriages: These men have plans to leave and they're putting them into action. They are no longer sharing a bed with their spouse. They are actively looking for a place to live, or filing for legal separation. These men might not talk much about leaving their marriages, as they are working toward resolving their problems, not mulling them over. Often, they say little but one day you find that they've moved out. In other words, they take action. This category is smaller than it should be—ideally, all men who are preparing for divorce would proceed in this fashion if they feel interest in a new woman, but it doesn't always happen that way.

So how do you tell the difference between a man who will leave and one who won't? A man who is serious about leaving will spend less time talking and complaining and more time taking action by doing things like finding a place to live and filling out divorce papers. Remember: people talk about their problems when they haven't resolved them yet. Men who are serious about divorce take action.

Almost all experts would suggest the same thing: until a man is actually separated, stay away from him. However, not everyone listens to the experts, and perhaps when you are armed with more information, you can make the decision for yourself. This chapter will cover some problems that you may encounter with these men, and provide some solutions for dealing with them.

The Three Problems with Soon-to-Be-Separated Men

While every relationship and every man is unique, here are the three main problems that you may encounter if you decide to become involved with a soon-to-be-separated man:

1. He's using you.
2. He isn't over his marriage.
3. He's a coward.

Problem 1: He's Using You

A soon-to-be-separated man who gets involved with another woman for support is using her. These men can generate compassion in others, especially from a woman who may be interested in him. If you meet one of these men, here are the types of things he will say about his marriage or wife:

- We don't love each other.
- We're miserable together.
- We were never meant to be together.
- We only got married for religious/financial/pregnancy reasons.
- She is abusive/mean/psychologically disturbed.
- She is uninterested in me sexually.
- She cheated on me.

In other words, he may try to appeal to your understanding. After all, who doesn't feel for someone who's suffering in a bad marriage? However, no matter how true these things are, he isn't telling them to you because they're true—he's telling you because he wants to absolve himself of guilt, and he wants you to believe that he's terribly unhappy or treated poorly so you will feel sorry for him and feel less hesitant about getting involved with him. In other words, he wants to use you to fill the void in his marriage. If you like this guy and feel glad that he seems ready to split, remember: a good man who's actually going to leave his wife will shut up and do so, and not use a relationship with another woman as a support system.

Despite any interest he has in you, he has nothing to offer you. If you have feelings for a soon-to-be-separated man, keep them to yourself and wait to see if he does something about his marital difficulties.

Problem 2: He Isn't Over His Marriage

This problem is one of the most common problems women face when dating men who've been married, whether separated, divorcing, or divorced. In these situations, the trick is figuring out if he's completed the grieving process or not. However, with soon-to-be-separated men, it's easy: he absolutely isn't over his marriage, period. **It is impossible to finish grieving a failed marriage if you're still in it.**

The next section on separated men details the signs that he isn't over his marriage. For the purposes of this section: the main confusion surrounding this particular problem is that women often misinterpret what "over" means. They assume a man is over his marriage because he wants a divorce, is unhappy, or doesn't love his wife anymore. They don't realize that things like guilt, fear of hurting her, money problems, fear of disapproval, and fear of hurting the children are all signs that he isn't over his marriage. Being "over" the marriage means he's completed much of the grieving process and has come to terms with many of the above-mentioned issues. A guy who hasn't even moved out clearly has not done that. For example:

꿈 When Lena met Kyle, he was looking to get divorced. He told her that his marriage had been over for two years. She asked why he hadn't left yet—he told her it was strictly financial, that he could not afford to live in a separate place. Lena thought that seemed reasonable, as Kyle seemed uninterested in his ex or his marriage, but she still kept her distance. Soon, Kyle received a promotion at work. In order to be with Lena, he moved out. Lena, happy that Kyle was going to proceed with his divorce, planned a nice dinner at his new place. However, when she arrived, Kyle wasn't in the mood to celebrate. He told Lena that his ex had started crying at his moving out, and he was wracked with guilt and wondering if he'd done the right thing.

So much for being "over" it. Lena's experience is a classic example of why soon-to-be-separated men are so risky—they aren't entirely honest with you because they aren't entirely honest with themselves. When a man stays in a lousy marriage for years and claims it's because of money, children, or other practical reasons, *he isn't being honest.*

Problem 3: He's a Coward

A man who thinks about getting divorced but hesitates to do so is certainly experiencing fear, but is not necessarily a coward. A divorce is a serious undertaking, and the decision to divorce is one of the most difficult decisions a person can make. However, there's a fine line between taking a decision seriously and avoiding a decision—a man who avoids getting divorced while seeking support from another woman is a coward.

Here are some signs of cowardly behavior:

- He tells you over and over how miserable his marriage is.
- He talks to you about wanting to leave, but doesn't follow through.
- He tells you he is actually going to leave, but then finds an excuse why he can't.
- He threatens to leave, and chickens out when his wife gets upset.
- He tells you he'll leave as long as you'll be there for him.

Remember: if he were ready to leave, he would have already. These guys don't have the courage to leave, and by involving themselves with another woman, they're either looking to make things more pleasant for themselves while they avoid their fears and stay stuck in an unhappy marriage, or hoping the other woman will give them the guts they lack. Even beyond the difficulties of involving yourself with a married man, his cowardly behavior may indicate problems that will cause difficulty in your own relationship.

The Three Rules for Dealing with Soon-to-Be-Separated Men

Now that you're acquainted with the problems that come with soon-to-be-separated men, here are some guidelines to follow:

1. Don't get involved.
2. Know his excuses.
3. Confront his behavior.

Rule 1: Don't Get Involved

There's nothing wrong with being interested in a soon-to-be-separated man; just keep your interest in your pocket for now, until he proves he's serious about divorcing and that he's emotionally ready to date. Avoiding involvement isn't just about right and wrong; it's about risk. Here are just some of the ways you can get hurt if you get involved with a man who hasn't separated yet.

He may never leave. If there was ever a chance he would actually leave his marriage, getting involved with him lowers that chance because he can avoid the unpleasant-ries that come along with separation while maintaining a relationship with you.

His ex will hate you. If his ex finds out, she will hate your guts and his too, and try to make you, him, and his divorce miserable. No matter how rotten the marriage was, she will blame you for the divorce and see you as a home-wrecker.

You won't trust him. Since he was willing to cheat on her, you'll eventually wonder if he'll do the same thing to you.

If you've already gotten involved with a soon-to-be-sepa-rated man, it's never too late to backpedal. Anyone can make a mistake—the important thing is that you correct the situ-ation and get yourself into a safe place.

Rule 2: Know His Excuses

There is one quality that all soon-to-be-separated men have in common: excuses for why they can't leave yet. Here is a list of common excuses:

- I don't want to hurt her.
- She will take everything from me.
- I can't afford to move out.
- I'll never see my children.
- It will hurt the children.
- My parents/religion taught me that divorce is wrong.

Some of these excuses are more valid than others, but there is only one real reason he hasn't left: *he's afraid to.*

Otherwise, he'd quit making excuses and just do it. Men who make excuses aren't ready to divorce, much less date.

Rule 3: Confront His Behavior

When a soon-to-be-separated man starts making excuses by trying to win your sympathy, or otherwise acts like a coward, confront him. Tell him what you see. This type of direct confrontation, especially from someone he likes, can accomplish two things:

1. It shows him you aren't to be trifled with.
2. It can give him the wake-up call he needs.

Men often respond to encouragement—thus, if you listen to his excuses, he may assume that they're working. But one blast from you should stop him in his tracks. The following are some confrontational responses you can give him if he begins to make excuses. Of course, the trick with confrontation is to stick by it—don't go back to listening to him again. Walk away to show that you mean it.

He says . . .	You respond . . .
I don't love her.	Then why don't you get divorced?
I never loved her.	Isn't it kind of mean to marry, and stay with, someone you don't love?
We were never meant to be together.	Then why are you?
We only got married for religious/financial/pregnancy reasons.	Then why are you still married?
She is abusive/mean/psychologically disturbed.	Why are you with someone like that?
She isn't interested in me sexually.	Have you addressed that in counseling?

He says . . .	You respond . . .
We only stay together for the kids.	Do you think the kids will like you dating other women?
It's over.	Does your wife know it's over? Will she mind you dating other women?
It's been over for X years.	Then why are you still married?

And, as always, you can use the general confrontation: "Stop complaining. Either get divorced or deal with it." Confrontation won't be easy. But rest assured, it's exactly what he needs. The good news: if he's any kind of man at all, he will respect you for being truthful with him.

THREE

The Separated Man

Imagine this scenario: You meet an interesting guy while sipping your latte at the local coffee house. He's cute and fun. He tells you that he's getting divorced, and you are secretly glad he's available. You begin dating, and eventually start sleeping together. You notice that he doesn't talk much about his divorce, but that he talks to his ex-wife regularly. After several months of this, you ask him when his divorce will be final, and he says he isn't sure, that he hasn't really begun the legal process of divorce yet.

How would you feel in this situation? More importantly, would you feel differently had he been able to give you a specific date? Chances are you would, as there is a difference between a man who is separated and a man who is getting divorced. The divorcing man has filed for divorce and is proceeding toward finalizing it; the separated man has not filed yet, and thus is not proceeding toward much of anything that would interest you. Although neither man is legally free yet, the divorcing man is moving in that direction in a concrete way, whereas the separated man is not. Thus, separated men have a whole host of issues that may come along with them.

Depending on the circumstances, dating experts either tell you to stay away from these men or act as if separated men are no different than other men. Most women will ignore the first guideline, and the second one is simply wrong. If you recall back to Chapter 1, relationships with separated men have a high Difficulty Index, which means that these relationships have much more potential for problems. This chapter will cover those problems, and provide guidelines on how to handle separated men.

Defining the Separated Man

A separated man lives in a separate residence from his spouse, but either has not filed for divorce or has filed but hasn't done anything to actually make the divorce happen. Unlike soon-to-be-separated men, where the boundaries are pretty clear (i.e., he's still married), the boundary situation becomes less clear with separated men. Unclear boundaries equal trouble. A separated man has broken off his marital relationship, but not only is he still legally married, he hasn't done anything to change that fact. Thus, whose man is he: yours or hers? This is another reason separated men have a high Difficulty Index (see Chapter 1).

Separated men fall into two categories: Waiting-to-See men and Can't-Be-Bothered men.

Waiting-to-See Men

A man in this category has separated from his spouse, usually recently, but has no concrete plans to divorce. He is waiting to see what will happen, and there is hope (whether great or small) that he will work things out with her. In other words: for him, the marriage is not really over.

Can't-Be-Bothered Men

This man has also separated from his spouse, but has not started dealing with the bother of legal divorce. Often, he'll have been separated for a while, even years, living a separate life from his ex and going about his business as if he were divorced. Sometimes a new relationship will prompt him to get on with it. However, what appears to be laziness can actually be fear, in that he avoids legal divorce because he fears losing money or fighting with his ex. Or, less often, he secretly hopes that things will work out between them.

What about Legal Separation?

Legal separation is when a separated couple files paperwork with the courts in order to legalize their separation and set child custody, financial, and other guidelines while they live apart. This is a way to protect all parties during separation. Most states recognize legal separation, but whether or not it's a requirement varies from state to state—in many states, one can proceed straight to divorce. Thus, a legally separated man is still only separated, can remain separated indefinitely, and can reunite with his wife at any time.

The Three Problems with Separated Men

While a myriad of problems can surface when one decides to start a relationship with a separated man, here are the three main problems that surround the men themselves:

1. He isn't over his marriage.
2. He is on the rebound.
3. Your relationship is limited.

Problem 1: He Isn't Over His Marriage

Most separated men are not over their marriages yet. Otherwise, they would get divorced. However, grief is tricky to spot in men. It's a rare man who will tell you "I'm not over my marriage yet!" A separated man may have been separated for a while, dislike his ex, and seek women to date, but still not be over his marriage. Why are grieving men hard to spot?

Grief isn't just about the ex. If you've never been divorced, it's easy to assume divorce is like a breakup—you miss your partner, then you move on. However, a separated man grieves his ex-wife and much more. He must also face a broken commitment, one that was intended to be permanent—remember: no one marries with the intention of getting divorced. If he has children, he may no longer live with them, and will see them less. He may have lost his home. That's a lot to lose. As a result, many women dating separated men come to realize that they're competing with his sense of failure, not his ex.

Men won't usually say they're grieving. For a man, to admit he isn't over his marriage is to admit weakness. Besides, he won't admit it to you because he knows you will probably run the other way. There's a decent chance he hasn't even admitted it to himself. Typically, men deal with grief differently than women do—it isn't uncommon to find them working a lot, playing more sports, even drinking more during tough times. Because of these sex differences, women may not recognize signs of grief in men.

Men don't wait to date. Men will often begin dating very quickly after separating, not because they're over it, but to help them *get* over it. Many men take a "get back in the game" approach to divorce because it makes them feel more like a problem-solver and less like a failure. They're often unaware that they may not be a good partner to a new woman. Women mistakenly assume a separated man must be "good to go" because he's dating or really attracted to them.

Grief is unpredictable. The only predictable aspect of grief is that it will occur when two people separate—but it is more difficult to know when, how, or for how long it will occur. Some men get over things quickly, while others may dwell in the past for years.

The key risks you face with a man who isn't over his marriage are that he could go back to his ex or, more likely, that he won't have enough to offer you. Investing time and energy in a man you care for just to find out he is still stuck in the past can be very unsettling and hurtful. Despite grief's unpredictable nature and men's different grieving style, there are ways to tell when a man isn't over his marriage yet:

SIGNS HE ISN'T OVER HIS MARRIAGE

Overinvolvement: He and his ex talk on the phone or have lunch frequently (exception: they have children together and keep their discussions pertaining to them); he goes to marital counseling with his ex "for her sake" or because "the courts said we should."

Helping: She calls him to discuss her problems; he fixes things at her place.

Fixation: He often talks about his ex and the marriage; he's still trying to figure out what went wrong in his marriage.

Admiration: He states how successful/gorgeous/great in bed his ex was.

Anger: He refuses to talk about his marriage; he bad-mouths his ex or blames her for the marriage ending.

Guilt: He lets his ex or kids get away with bad behavior, or overindulges them; he feels responsible for the separation.

Procrastination: He avoids divorce paperwork.

Freudian slips: He accidentally calls you by his ex-wife's name.

Although not signs per se, there are three more factors you should consider, because each of them is very likely to coincide with grief:

- He is very recently separated.
- His ex ended the marriage.
- His ex cheated on him.

Carrie and Zack lived in the same town, and met at the local coffee house. Zack's wife, after years of a bad marriage, had taken his children and left him a few months earlier. Carrie, who ran her own business, was single, good-looking, and fun. She was nothing like Zack's wife, who was unhappy and didn't take good care of herself. Carrie and Zack hit it off, and began dating and then sleeping together. Soon Carrie wanted to move things forward with Zack, but he wasn't ready, as he was waiting to see what his wife was going to do. Truthfully, Zack was hoping his wife would come back. Carrie stopped seeing Zack.

Zack, a Waiting-to-See man, wasn't over his marriage. Despite all the signs that the marriage was over (e.g., his wife had left him), he procrastinated on filing for divorce because he wasn't ready to let go. Thus, Carrie pursued a relationship with a man who appeared available but really wasn't.

Even though the legal bond of marriage may seem like a mere annoyance, it can be a security blanket protecting him from whatever he fears: officially ending his marriage, financial ruin, moving on with a new woman, etc. Every separated man I've known has had something holding him back from divorcing, and has kept his relationships casual. Thus, be very cautious when dating these men.

Problem 2: He Is on the Rebound

Rebounding is when a person looks to a new relationship to fill the void left by a recently ended relationship. Men are more likely to rebound than women. Why is this? Men often have fewer ways to fill the void left by a breakup than women do, as women tend to talk with friends, family, and therapists about the breakup. Men, who typically confide in a wife or girlfriend, don't always have people to talk to when a breakup occurs, and they aren't as willing to go to therapy. Further, according to John Gray, author of *Men Are from Mars, Women Are from Venus,* men, unlike women, don't like to chew on problems, they like to solve them, and therefore may begin to pursue women soon after a breakup.

The possibility of rebounding is greatest with recent splits, which means separated and divorcing men are the most risky. Many of these men have sat in unsatisfying marriages for years and are eager for a new woman, for companionship, for sex. They are also looking for support, validation, and a sense of feeling wanted. This puts you at risk of being the "transitional woman," and the closer you are to his separation, the higher the risk. If you are seeing a divorcing man, here are ten signs he may be on the rebound:

TEN SIGNS HE IS ON THE REBOUND

1. He's recently separated (usually less than six months ago or so).
2. He seems to really like you even though you hardly know one another (for example, he constantly compliments you or calls you all the time).
3. He seems enamored with you even though you have little in common.
4. He tells you how superior you are to his ex and how much better you are for him.
5. Your looks or behavior greatly resemble his ex.
6. Your looks or behavior are the complete opposite of his ex.
7. He downplays any connection to his marriage (for example, he tells you he never really loved his ex, that they haven't had sex in years, that she's an ugly ogre, etc.).
8. He tells you his divorce will be quick and easy (they often aren't).
9. He comes on strong, then backs off once you show interest.
10. He is "on the prowl," seeking out lots of women to date.

If you like him, his attention and adoration will feel really nice. Yet, what happens in rebound relationships is that a man reaches out to a woman to fulfill his long unmet needs. Once some of them are met, he realizes he is either not ready for a relationship or you aren't his type—and then he splits. These men are often unaware that they don't have a lot to offer a woman yet; they only know how good it feels to have the support they've needed.

🕊 Melinda and Todd met at work. Todd, a separated man, was charming and complimentary to Melinda. He told her how pretty she was and clamored to take her out. He was very attentive and called her all the time; she began to like him and show interest in him. After a few dates, Todd's attentions waned. Melinda asked him what happened, and he said he didn't want to "get serious." Later, Melinda heard that Todd had been chasing all the young women at the office, and he continued to hit on Melinda occasionally to see if she would respond to his advances.

Todd, a rebounder, wanted any woman who would give him a sense of immediate validation.

Problem 3: Your Relationship Is Limited

A separated man is a man in limbo. No matter how long he's been separated and no matter how he's gone on with his life, he still retains an important bond with his ex. In a practical sense, they are still legal partners who share all the legal benefits (and drawbacks) of marriage, including shared income, shared debts, shared property, etc. If one partner decides to spend a bunch of money or sell the house, it affects the other partner.

🕊 Jeff has been separated for four years, and has not filed for divorce. During his separation, Jeff moved out of state, got a new job, and began a new life. He sends his wife money from time to time, but otherwise has little to do with her. An entrepreneur who has done well for himself, Jeff fears divorce and the possibility of having to give up half of his businesses and earnings. He dates women, but never gets seriously involved with any of them.

Jeff is a Can't-Be-Bothered man—he doesn't want to bother with the legal and financial hassles that can come with divorce. Jeff's relationships with women never get serious because the relationships have nowhere to go.

When you date a separated man, in some ways you're dating a married man. Even if he has no desire to reunite with his spouse, the legal remnants of the marriage remain. This creates unclear boundaries in the relationship, where he is essentially involved with two women. He is not ready for a serious relationship, and marriage is impossible because he is still married. Thus, the relationship can't proceed beyond dating and casual involvement. If you want more than that, you will have to walk away unless he's prepared to get divorced.

Even if the separated man decides to move forward with divorce, he still has an entire divorce to contend with. Divorce is usually a long and complicated process. Most states only require three to six months to finalize a divorce, but it usually takes a year or two because of conflicts. Thus, if you meet a man who is separated and it takes him some time to begin the divorce process, you may spend the first two years of your relationship with a man who isn't legally free. And if that isn't enough to swallow, his divorce could come with conflict, stress, an angry ex-wife, and other annoyances that can really chip away at your happiness and your relationship. Thus, think hard about investing much in a separated man.

The Three Rules for Dating Separated Men

Now that you're acquainted with the problems that come with separated men, how do you proceed? Here are some guidelines for dating and relationships with these men:

1. Ask plenty of questions as soon as possible.
2. Know what his excuses mean.
3. Keep it casual.

Rule 1: Ask Plenty of Questions as Soon as Possible

When dating, people don't often volunteer information about themselves that will make them appear less desirable. Thus, asking questions is extremely important. When you meet a man you are interested in, you may feel hesitant to ask too many personal questions for fear that he won't like your questions—or that you won't like his answers. However, asking a few key questions now can save you a lot of pain later. It can also prevent this annoying conversation:

You: "Why didn't you tell me you haven't even filed for divorce yet?"

Him: "You never asked."

Most men will answer your questions truthfully, as long as you ask. Otherwise, he won't volunteer anything that might make him look bad in any way. Remember: men want to impress women.

Here are some questions you must ask a separated man within the first few dates:

When he filed for divorce. You will need to ask this in order to know that he is separated. He either has not filed, has filed but done nothing to follow it up, or has only filed for legal separation.

When he and his spouse separated. A man who's recently separated is different from one who's been separated for years. The recently separated man may be preparing to divorce, but he may also be a Waiting-to-See man. The man who has been separated for a long time (for over a year) is probably a Can't-Be-Bothered man. The

Can't-Be-Bothered man may be further along in the griev-ing process, but failure to close the deal is still a red flag.

What his ex thinks about the separation. You may or may not get a straight answer to this question. However, if they are not divorced, the answer is probably clear—she doesn't like the idea of divorce. If she wanted to divorce him, she'd have already done so.

Why he isn't moving forward. This may seem like too personal a question to ask on the first few dates, but think about it: What man really expects a woman to be satisfied with a guy who's essentially still married? You deserve to know what you're getting into, or the deal is off.

ADVICE FOR ASKING QUESTIONS
Asking personal questions isn't easy, so here are a few tips:

Break the ice. To start things off, you might ask him if he's ever been married. If he says yes, you can proceed to when the divorce was finalized, and work from there. If you are already somewhat acquainted with him, you can more easily launch into more specific questions.

Be respectful, even if you don't like what you hear. A man who tells you the truth about himself is giving you a gift: the ability to make an informed choice about how to proceed. If you bust his chops, the chances of his being honest with you, or any other woman, decrease in the future. And keep your tone of voice neutral, as if you are curious about him, rather than interrogating him.

Ask specific questions. For example, a man tells you he's getting divorced. Ask him when he filed for divorce instead of asking when his divorce began. His answer determines your next move: if he hasn't filed, you know to stop seeing him, or to expect little from him. If he already filed, you might continue to see him, watching closely to see if he proceeds with the divorce. If you assume "getting divorced" means "filed papers," you risk getting more involved than you wanted to. Remember: men, like all people, are more likely to tell you the truth if you ask a direct question.

Expect the truth. You may wonder if you have the right to ask such personal questions. The answer is yes: you deserve to know anything that would influence your decision to date this guy. However, some men may evade your questions. If you ask a specific question, you should get a specific answer. If you don't, he's trying to avoid admitting something he knows you won't like. Difficult as it is, ask again: he will either get angry or answer. Either way, you get the information you need. If you ever catch him in a lie, dump him.

Rule 2: Know His Excuses

Men who procrastinate on filing for divorce will have plenty of excuses. And many of these excuses will sound reasonable. Take another look at "Rule 2: Know His Excuses" in the previous chapter. It may look like a list of excuses, but it's really a list of fears. Yes, the procrastinating separated man is *afraid* to get divorced. Will he admit to that? Doubtful. In fact, he will probably deny it. Moreover, most of the excuses, like "I can't afford a divorce" and "I don't have time for all that paperwork," are not insurmountable in nature, and others, such as "I'll never see my children again," are untrue except in the most extreme cases. But ultimately, the real issue for you is that you can't compete with something as powerful as fear. If he won't face his fears and get divorced, don't bother with him.

Rule 3: Keep It Casual

If you still feel comfortable dating a separated man, then do so. Just don't expect much from him or from the relationship, don't give much, and remember that he could get back together with his wife. Here are some tips on how to keep this relationship casual:

Continue seeing other men. Why should a man who can't break his commitment get yours? He should know that if he wants to be with you, he has to prove he's good enough. Until then, you're a free agent. Meanwhile, you'll be out having fun, and may even find a more interesting man who's actually unencumbered by the annoyances of a marital contract!

Don't give him sex. He should earn the right to have sex with you, just as he should earn your commitment. If he's getting sex, he will have less of an incentive to move forward. And don't let anyone, especially him, tell you that this is playing games—wanting to protect yourself from giving more than you get in return isn't playing games, it's looking out for Number One. However, if you aren't concerned about a future with this man and don't mind that your relationship remains casual, then have sex with him when you feel comfortable doing so. Just be careful that you don't start expecting him to change.

Don't play shrink. If he has the audacity to discuss his marital problems and breakup pain with you, cut him off. He should leave that stuff for his buddies, family, or therapist. It's important to ask questions in order to find out where he is emotionally, but don't listen to his problems or try to advise him in any way. This applies even if he wants to move forward with divorce and needs a "push"—don't be the one to give it to him, no matter how much you want to be with him. Think about it: which man sounds better, the man who embarks on divorce because you urge him to or the man who embarks on divorce all on his own?

If you find yourself in a relationship with a separated man who won't get on with his divorce, it's never too late to back off. Just walk away, and tell him to call you when he gets divorced.

Separated men (as well as soon-to-be-separated men) are experiencing difficult times and deserve all the support they can get. However, they should get that support from their friends, family, or a therapist, and *not* from a new woman. It isn't wrong for these men to want to date, but they should be completely up front about where they are, and should not try to pass themselves off as free and unencumbered when they aren't. They should keep a woman away from their marital mess, and clean it up on their own time. Then the women who date these men can make an informed choice, knowing what they're getting into.

There are soon-to-be-separated and separated men who handle their dating lives respectfully. But not all of them do, and this is one of the reasons why separated men have a high Difficulty Index (see Chapter 1). Separated men are not an easy bunch to date, so use the tools outlined in this chapter in order to increase your chances of success with these men. Remember, the ultimate goal is to be happy.

FOUR

Single, Married, or What?
The Divorcing Man

Compared to all the men presented in this book thus far, the divorcing man presents the biggest quandary when it comes to dating. The term *divorcing* refers to a man who has moved out, has filed for divorce, and is proceeding with his divorce. Men who have not completed these steps (a.k.a. separated men) are covered in previous chapters. Like the separated man, the divorcing man's money and property still belong to another woman, even if his marital relationship is over. However, unlike the separated man, the divorcing man is proceeding with divorce, which implies that there is a potential future with him.

What do you do?

Is It Okay to Date a Divorcing Man?

If you ask ten different people this question, you will get ten different answers. However, most of the answers fall into two camps: the "Stay Away" camp and the "Fair Game" camp. The Stay Away camp includes a few dating experts; they emphasize that divorcing men have not sufficiently recovered from their marriages and have little to offer a woman. Others in this camp feel that until his divorce is finalized, he is a married man and therefore off limits. These folks view the *legal bond* as the defining aspect of marriage. In contrast, the Fair Game camp takes a relationship-centered approach to divorce, and views the *marital relationship*, not the legal bond, as the defining aspect of marriage. In other words, once his marital relationship ends, then he is fair game.

For the Fair Gamers, the rationale is that marriage is *first* a relationship, *then* a legal agreement. Picture an orange: an orange has delicious fruit plus a protective peel. The peel plays an important role, but without the fruit, it is no longer an orange. It is the same with marriage—the legal agreement provides protection for the marital relationship, but once the marital relationship is over, only the legal "peel" remains. Moreover, regardless of which camp you belong to, a man who dates during his divorce is not "cheating"—he cannot cheat on someone he is no longer committed to. This does not mean that dating a divorcing man isn't complicated. Even though divorcing men are free to date, they come with a lot of baggage, and relationships with these men tend have a low probability for happiness.

This chapter is especially important for two reasons:

1. As long as he's ended his marital relationship, you should be able to date a divorcing man if you want to. However, if you choose to do so, you will need guidance.
2. These relationships can succeed—this chapter will increase the chances of that happening.

Is Dating a Divorcing Man the Same as Dating a Divorced Man?

The answer to this question is a resounding *No*—it's much more difficult. Although several of the problems and challenges of divorcing men are similar to those of divorced men, there are two important differences. First, many of the problems that come with men who've been married before are *much more likely to occur* if he is still getting divorced. Additionally, divorcing men come with extra challenges that divorced men do not. In the world that single women are used to, a man is either single or partnered—when he and his partner break up, he is free. Divorcing men are unique— they are without a relationship partner, but they still have a legal partner. Thus, if you have a relationship with a divorcing man, the boundaries of that relationship are unclear. Unclear boundaries equal trouble. Divorced men, despite their baggage, are legally free, providing a clearer boundary between him and his former life.

If you develop an interest in a divorcing man, you need to be aware of the problems women encounter in these relationships. The more quickly you can identify problems, the more easily you can solve them. The following section details the six problems that often accompany divorcing men, and in the next chapter, I tackle the six rules for dating these men.

The Six Problems with Divorcing Men

Of course, every divorcing man is different. However, there are some problems that continually surface among them. The six problems that tend to occur with many divorcing men are the following:

1. He isn't over his marriage.
2. He isn't interested in an actual relationship.
3. He wants to hide your relationship.
4. Others disapprove of your relationship.
5. There are delays in the divorce proceedings.
6. You have to "share" him.

Problem 1: He Isn't Over His Marriage

Unresolved grief can plague any previously married man, but the risk is much greater if he is still getting divorced. This is the problem you are most likely to encounter when dating a divorcing man. A divorcing man may want his divorce, know that his ex is not right for him, and seek women to date, but still not be over his marriage. The male grieving process is covered in greater detail in Chapter 3.

The interesting, and confusing, aspect of the grief process during divorce is that it is highly variable. Although there will be a legal record of when his divorce is final, the so-called "psychological divorce" can occur years before, or after, legal divorce. A newly divorcing man may have already processed much of his loss, and a man who has been divorcing for a year may still be grieving.

In addition to the general warning signs listed in Chapter 3, here are some warning signs of grief to look for in a divorcing man:

- He still says "wife" instead of "ex-wife."
- Although he's filed for divorce, he procrastinates on moving forward with it.
- He quibbles with his ex over minor divorce details, such as who gets to keep the bathroom rug, the ugly lamp they never used, or the unused shampoo.

🐾 When Jake met Moira, his divorce, initiated by his ex, was nearly final. Although Jake was caring and fun, he often talked about his ex and still referred to her as "my wife." Once, while in bed together, Moira expressed some shyness over her freckles. Jake replied kindly that she needn't worry, his wife had lots of freckles too and they were something he'd always loved about her. Soon after, Jake started calling Moira less. Jake and his ex did not get back together, but it was clear he was not over her yet. As a result, despite the fact that Jake and Moira got along well, he had little to offer her at that time.

🐾 Unlike Jake, Marc and his ex clashed and he didn't miss her at all. However, he harbored feelings of guilt about their divorce. Marc had cheated on his wife, which ended their marriage, leaving him with every-other-weekend parenting time with his two-year-old son. He took responsibility for his role in the demise of the marriage. However, Marc worked all the time and kept himself very busy, and the few women he dated came and went. Eventually, as the divorce was ending, he admitted that he missed his old life—not the *reality* of his ex, but the *idea* of having their family unit united once more. Marc had not quite forgiven himself and was still processing his loss. This went on for years; eventually he was ready to pursue a lasting relationship.

When you date a divorcing man, you have to pay close attention to what he says and does. He may say, and even believe, that he's "over it," but the signs will tell you otherwise. Just as importantly, trust your instincts. Think about the last time a man said something amiss—you probably felt something wasn't quite right, but you didn't know why. For example, your date comments that his ex is extremely attractive. You feel weird that he said it, but then you let it go because you don't want to look jealous or petty. Later, you realize that it really isn't a good sign for a man to brag about his ex—especially to a date!

Some signs, like taking her calls or referring to her as "wife," can also be old habits he needs to change. And he may show *occasional* anger, guilt, or confusion about his former marriage. A certain amount of processing of the past is normal and can recur for years. But there's a difference between occasionally thinking about the past and being stuck in the past—the first won't affect your relationship, but the second will. *If you aren't sure, examine your relationship: if you have doubts, they are probably justified.*

This is a good reason to take things slowly with divorcing men. If you begin to suspect the man you are dating isn't over his marriage, stop dating him. Tell him why—he probably won't like hearing it, but it should make him think. Your backing off encourages him to deal with unresolved issues; continuing to date him will not only make you unhappy, but will make him even less inclined to get over the past. If he works through his grief, you can reconsider him.

Problem 2:
He Isn't Interested in an Actual Relationship

Another risk you face when dating a divorcing man is that he may not want a relationship. The potential reasons why are too numerous to list here, and for your purposes the reason doesn't matter—what matters is that he isn't interested in a real relationship and you will be wasting your time if you want one. Here are five signs to look for:

- He's ambivalent. He seems interested, then doesn't; you spend time together, then don't hear from him for a week or two; he makes dates and then breaks them; he says he will call and then doesn't; and/or he calls infrequently.

- The relationship does not progress beyond the dating stage. You don't start spending more time together or experience increased closeness in the relationship over time.
- He seems more interested in sex than anything else.
- You want more time together, affection, or intimacy than he does.
- He says he isn't looking to get serious. You'd be surprised how many women don't take a statement like this seriously, or think they can change this mindset.

As with the man who isn't over his marriage, his lack of interest in a relationship won't always stop him from dating and getting involved with you on some level; he may desire companionship and/or sex because he hasn't had either in a long time.

The tricky part is that he won't necessarily admit, or even realize, that he isn't interested in more. If you like this man, it's natural to want to move forward with the relationship. Too often, women don't realize that these men aren't looking for a relationship until they have given a lot of themselves, only to feel hurt, angry, or used. Solution? *Take things slowly—don't sleep with him or invest much in the relationship until he proves that his interest level is as great as yours and consistent over time.*

Problem 3: He Wants to Hide Your Relationship

It is not uncommon for divorcing men to try to keep their romances clandestine. Some lawyers will advise their clients to do so as well. Dating during divorce is not illegal, but it can create considerable jealousy and anger in his ex, thereby threatening any settlement he is trying to negotiate with her. If he has children, it can make their lives more difficult, which in turn looks bad with courts and custody evaluators.

The more casual your relationship, and the earlier he is in his divorce process, the more discretion you should use. Giving his ex, kids, and family some time to process the divorce before exposing them to a new woman is better for everyone, including you—if he introduces you too soon, you may wind up the object of their resentment.

However, if your relationship becomes serious and certainly if you begin planning your future together, secrecy is no longer acceptable—if he gets the privilege of a committed relationship with you, then he can be a man and own up to it. Don't make a commitment to a man who insists on hiding you. You're tolerating enough by dating a man who isn't divorced yet—why add insult to injury?

✌ Laura began dating David soon after he left his eight-year marriage. They kept their relationship quiet for several months. First, David told his parents about Laura; eventually, they wanted to meet her in person. Then David told his son Cole about Laura; Cole seemed open to meeting her and liked her when he met her. David also told his ex about Laura, preferring her to find out from him rather than from others. But David's ex was furious that Cole spent time with Laura, and tried in court to legally prevent Laura from being around the boy. Even David's lawyer encouraged David to keep Cole away from Laura, so the ex would calm down. However, because David and Laura were serious as a couple and Cole liked Laura, and since Laura made sure Cole got plenty of one-on-one time with David, the courts did nothing to prevent Cole from seeing Laura. Even the custody evaluator, recognizing that Cole was not negatively influenced by Laura's presence, expressed no disapproval.

Problem 4: Others Disapprove of Your Relationship

Not everyone feels the same about dating during divorce. If you are dating a divorcing man, your relationship may evoke disapproving opinions, whether you want to hear them or not. Disapproval can be annoying, even upsetting. However, disapproval is much more complicated than it appears. Disapprovers will often state why they disapprove, but behind that STATED reason is a more compelling REAL reason, which they won't likely acknowledge to themselves, much less to you. Here are some examples:

Friends: Friends will probably support you because they're mostly concerned with your happiness. But you may have one friend who wishes you'd find a "free" man.
- *Stated reason for disapproval:* Dating a man who isn't divorced yet
- *Real reason:* Fear that you will get hurt

The courts: Most judges won't care that he is dating you. The exception: If he has children, courts will frown if he's introduced them to multiple women, if you bad-mouth their mother to them, or if you do anything that could be construed as harmful to them.
- *Stated reason for disapproval:* His dating during divorce
- *Real reason:* Fear for the children's welfare

His ex: The strongest disapproval will likely come from her. This is especially true if he left her, but can happen no matter what the situation. Even if she was open to the divorce, seeing him with another woman may trigger jealousy.
- *Stated reason for disapproval:* His choosing to divorce her; his dating during divorce; his having begun dating "so soon"; you honing in on "her husband"

- *Real reason:* Pain at the loss of her marriage; feelings of rejection and inadequacy; fear that you have more going for you than she does

His parents: His parents may not like his divorcing or his seeing you, especially if they are old-fashioned or religious. They may grapple with how his divorce affects them, their relationship with his ex, and time with their grandchildren. Parents who haven't been divorced may not understand, and those who have may be unpleasantly reminded of their own painful divorces.
- *Stated reason for disapproval:* Their son choosing to divorce; his dating during divorce; his having begun dating "so soon"
- *Real reason:* Fear their son will regret divorcing or get hammered in the divorce; fear they will see their grandchildren less; fear that his divorce reflects poor parenting on their part; if religious, fear that their divorcing son is sinning

Church: Most churches do not support divorce, much less dating during one. If he or his family belongs to a church, you can bet he was discouraged from divorcing, no matter how bad his marriage was.
- *Stated reason for disapproval:* Divorce is wrong and/or not sanctioned by God
- *Real reason:* Fear they will lose a member of their flock; fear they didn't do an adequate job teaching or guiding him

You: Strange as it sounds, you may be your greatest critic. When Shannon was dating divorcing man Scott, she experienced no disapproval from anyone but herself. Shannon hated admitting to people that Scott wasn't divorced yet, and part of her felt like it was "wrong" to date him.

- *Stated reason for disapproval:* Dating a divorcing man
- *Real reason:* Fear that you aren't a "moral" person

When you examine the stated reasons for disapproval among any of these people, they all refer to *someone besides themselves*: *he* is getting divorced, *you* are dating a divorcing man, etc. When you examine their real reasons, they refer to something *within themselves*—usually painful feelings. Note how often the words *fear* and *pain* appear. In other words, disapprovers typically claim that their disapproval is about your actions, when it's really about their internal feelings.

꽃 Carlos, after being married to an alcoholic for nine years, moved out and filed for divorce. He met Monique at a local teacher's conference. Carlos received criticism from two people: his ex-wife and an old church friend. Both chastised him for divorcing, and his ex angrily told Monique to stay away from "her husband." Their *stated* reason for disapproval: divorce is wrong, period. However, Carlos's ex was devastated by his leaving, and felt betrayed that he'd moved on with another woman. Carlos's disapproving friend, left by his own spouse years before, had never forgiven her for leaving him. The *real* reason for their disapproval was not religion, or right and wrong; it was their own unresolved feelings of pain and betrayal.

꽃 Catherine, while dating her divorcing boyfriend Alex (who had a child from his previous marriage), was surprised (and hurt) that Alex's parents were distant with her, especially considering that they were not fond of Alex's ex-wife. They told Alex they didn't approve of his dating while still divorcing. Alex's parents were old-fashioned, and many people, including Alex's ex, were pressuring them to encourage Alex to give the marriage one more try. Alex's parents had nothing against Catherine, but were torn between wanting their son to be happy and believing he should stay married "for better and for worse." Over time, they accepted Alex's choice and warmed up to Catherine.

It's normal to feel hurt and angry when you experience disapproval. Here are some ways to help you handle disapproval:

- Talk with friends or a therapist, and try to work through the feelings.
- Don't get caught up in stated reasons for disapproval—try to identify the real reasons. Once you do, you will feel more compassion and less anger.
- Don't feel you must defend or explain yourself to a disapprover. This puts too much emphasis on their stated reasons, instead of focusing on the real ones. Gently mention possible real reasons to the disapprover, rather than trying to convince the person they're wrong. They will resist at first, but it will give them something to think about.
- Be clear about your own beliefs about divorce, and about dating a divorcing man. Once you know exactly where you stand, you won't feel as compelled to defend yourself.
- If the disapproval comes from people related to your man (his parents, his ex), they should discuss their feelings with him, not you. This important boundary should be introduced, and reinforced, by him.

Remember, no woman wants to date a divorcing man. Rather, she has found a man she cares for, and must therefore tolerate his divorce. If you've met a man special enough to endure waiting for his divorce to end, then it makes no sense to say "See you in a year or two," simply because the relationship makes some other people uncomfortable. If you experience disapproval, follow the advice here and give it time. Eventually, their disapproval, and your discomfort with it, will wane.

Problem 5:
There Are Delays in the Divorce Proceedings

Most divorces take longer than they should. Although most states require only three to six months for two agreeable people to divorce, most divorcing couples aren't that agreeable. More conflict equals longer divorce. A divorce takes one to two years on average, and can take much longer. Other factors that slow down a divorce process include overloaded courts, busy or contentious attorneys, children (i.e., custody battles), and old-fashioned divorce laws. Although many states now have "no fault" divorce legislation, others still attempt to determine who was at fault in the marriage.

> ✍ Lorna looked forward to the end of her boyfriend Joe's divorce—the final hearing was scheduled for the first week in July. In April, the ex's lawyer said he was not available that week in July—the next available date wasn't until October. When October came, her lawyer claimed he hadn't had sufficient time to prepare, and wanted more time!

If you are dating a divorcing man, you are eager for his divorce to finalize. He may claim that his divorce will be quick or is almost over. More often than not, divorcing men say these things because they want them to be true, not because they are. If true, you'll see for yourself very quickly. Otherwise, be prepared for his divorce to take one to two years, and expect delays. In the meantime, go on with your lives and continue to work on your relationship.

Problem 6: You Have to "Share" Him

A divorcing man has no relationship partner, but still has a legal partner. This introduces a third party into your relationship. Unfortunately, until the divorce ends, in some ways you must share him with another woman. This creates unclear boundaries because he has obligations to two women, when there should only be one. One of the most basic needs we have in our relationships is fidelity—we want our partners to be *ours*. This isn't possessiveness; it's human nature. Therefore, because a divorcing man still belongs to another in some ways, that basic need isn't met. Here are examples of how you will have to "share" your divorcing man:

His property is still legally hers. This includes his money, belongings, home, and cars. In this arena, his ex has much more power than you do. He cannot spend much money on you, or whisk you off to Europe. And don't get attached to anything—he could lose any of his assets when the divorce is finalized.

He may have to support her. If his ex is unemployed, he may have to pay all her bills during the divorce.

Some of his time is hers. He will have to invest time and energy in severing the legal ties to his ex. In this way, he must still focus on her.

You can't move in together. Legally you can, but it has the potential to create problems for you and your relationship, especially if he has children (see the next chapter).

Under normal circumstances, you and he dictate when to move in together—with a divorcing man, his marital status influences your choice.

You can't get married. This probably won't be an important issue unless his divorce drags on interminably. But, again, it's an infringement upon freedoms you would normally take for granted.

These issues may not concern you in the early stages of your relationship. But as you grow closer and become more involved in each other's lives, you will become increasingly uncomfortable that his finances and life still involve another woman. Follow the advice in this chapter, talk with friends or a good therapist when you need to, and remind yourself that this is *temporary*.

An important point: You only have to share him in the legal sense. The limitations listed previously are dictated by the realities of divorce. If your relationship advances to the committed stage, sharing him should not include him:

- Having regular phone conversations or visits with his ex, except what is needed for dealing with children or divorce-related business
- Allowing her a key to his home or car
- Performing home or car repairs for her
- Spending birthdays or holidays with her (even if they have children)

These are friendly behaviors, but they aren't appropriate when he's committed to you. Talk to him about it; if he resists letting go of the past, move on.

FIVE

The Six Rules for Dating Divorcing Men

Now that you're acquainted with the problems that come with divorcing men, how do you proceed? Here are some guidelines for dating and relationships with these men:

1. Ask plenty of questions as soon as possible.
2. Take things slowly.
3. Keep your own life, friends, and activities.
4. Stay on the periphery of his divorce.
5. Avoid competing with the ex.
6. Accept the limitations of the relationship.

Rule 1: Ask Plenty of Questions as Soon as Possible

As stated in Chapter 3, learning to ask questions is important when dating, because people don't often volunteer information about themselves that will make them appear less desirable. With divorcing men, you will have to ask questions you've probably never asked before. Knowing as much as possible up front allows you to make good choices and prevent problems down the road. The following are the things you must find out within the first few dates.

If he's been married, and when his divorce was finalized. Because you won't often find out that your date is still getting divorced until you ask *both* of these questions, ask these questions first.

When he filed for divorce. Ask this if and when you find out he's not officially divorced yet. The question within the question is whether he's filed at all—filing of divorce papers is perhaps the most important sign that a man is serious about divorce.

How long he's been separated. The longer he's been separated, the higher the probability that he is ready to move on and that he and his ex and kids have begun working through the grief process—and the less time you have to spend dating a divorcing man. A man who is early in his separation is a red flag, so proceed with great caution.

How long he's lived on his own. This is to make sure he lives in his own place. Divorcing couples may cohabit if money is tight, or refuse to give up turf because they fear losing the house or the kids if they leave. Even with good reasons, and even if he's sleeping on the couch, a man still living with his "ex" is not in a position to date. If he's serious about moving on with his life, he'll find a way to move out.

If he has children. Children usually mean a longer and more contentious divorce. And if your relationship works out, you must face a host of issues. This is discussed in detail in Chapter 10.

Who initiated the divorce, and why. Initially, you probably won't get the whole answer, but you can glean a lot by what he does tell you. If he wanted the divorce, he's more ready to move on. However, the woman he left won't be as ready as he is to move on, posing a potential problem for him and eventually for you. On the other hand, if she initiated divorce proceedings, he will more than likely be grieving and not be an ideal date. If cheating was involved (his or hers), bitterness often results. If he blames her for the divorce, or has no clue why things ended, stay away.

The last time he had sex with his ex. This is very personal, but if you can find this out, it can tell you volumes. If he hasn't had sex in years, this guy can sit through the bad times. If they had sex after they separated (or worse, even more recently), that's a serious red flag. One-third of couples sleep together after separation or divorce—the reasons for this are beyond the scope of the book, but it's a common (and unhealthy) way to stay connected with an ex. You want a man who's moved on, and sleeping with her is a clear sign he hasn't. This question requires a greater level of familiarity between him and you, so don't ask too soon.

𝕵❧ Samantha met Paul through a group of colleagues. Paul really liked Samantha, so he didn't volunteer right away that he had just begun the divorce process and hadn't filed his papers yet. Paul had processed much of the loss of his marriage years before, and was embarrassed about his situation; he feared Samantha would judge him. Samantha felt comfortable asking questions, and although Paul was nervous, he answered them all truthfully. Samantha wasn't happy about his marital status, but knowing the truth up front helped her protect herself. Once Paul filed his papers and showed he was serious about divorcing, they began to date.

Asking personal questions may be awkward, but it's crucial. See Chapter 3 for advice on how to ask men personal questions.

Rule 2: Take Things Slowly

If taking things slowly is useful in any new relationship, it's crucial when dating a divorcing man. Because of the inherent risks in this type of relationship, you should resist proceeding at the pace you normally would. Here are some guidelines.

Don't have sex too soon. Who wants to get sexually involved with a man just to find out he's on the rebound, going back to his ex, or really not interested in a relationship right now? These are all significant risks with divorcing men. The longer you wait, the more you will learn whether he's worth getting involved with. This process takes *months*, not days or weeks.

Don't commit too soon. If you hit it off with a man, it's natural to get involved and become exclusive as a couple. This type of commitment has its costs and rewards, and committing too soon to a divorcing man means greater Input and less Output (see Chapter 1 on Input and Output). Before making any commitment, take several months to evaluate him and his situation—the more complicated things are, the longer you should try to wait.

Don't move in with him. If a divorcing man wants to move in with you to get out of his marital home, say No. This is rescuing him, not loving him, and will hurt you down the road. If his divorce is progressing and your relationship has gotten serious, moving in together will be a more natural desire. However, waiting until the divorce is over to move in together lessens the chance that problems will arise. If he has children, moving in with him places you in a parentlike role before the children (and you) are ready. This is tough on everyone, and courts frown on it. Also, living together will provide no escape from the stress of dating a divorcing man, thus taking further toll on your happiness and on your relationship. In other words, this is a Low Output situation. It's frustrating to wait—but some frustration is better than the trouble you will face if you don't.

Don't meet his kids too soon. If he has children, they are adjusting to stressful changes in their lives. Never meet his kids until you are serious as a couple. Meeting their dad's new partner too soon may upset them, and if you split up, will cause them more confusion and feelings of loss. Courts and custody evaluators put the children's needs first. Be sure to take your time meeting them, and proceed very slowly.

Rule 3: Keep Your Own Life, Friends, and Activities

One of the most misery-making mistakes you can make when dating a divorcing man is to devote yourself to the relationship and lose track of your life. With a nondivorcing man, making your relationship your life can lead to unhappiness—no relationship can meet all of your needs and a relationship with a divorcing man meets even fewer of your needs, putting your happiness (and relationship) at even greater risk. The solution? Stay independent and committed to your own life.

Here are some tips:

Keep your job. Work means that you are financially independent and have something important in your life other than your relationship. Men often use their jobs to distract them from their problems, and you can do the same if things get tough.

Spend lots of time with friends. Some women tend to blow off their friendships when they get involved in a relationship. This is a bad idea in general, but disastrous when dating a divorcing man. You will need your friends to talk to during tough times, which prevents you from venting on your man and creating more strain on your relationship. Plus, friends are another way that you stay independent and happy, and they remind you that you have a life that's worthwhile if things don't work out with your relationship.

Have lots of activities. You should always keep some hobbies and/or activities in your life—these things give your life meaning and enjoyment so that your every happiness does not depend upon your divorcing man. Also, until your relationship becomes serious, you will want to make your own plans for holidays—the divorcing man may be spending holidays with his kids or his extended family.

Keep your finances separate. Don't mingle finances or give a divorcing man money, for two reasons. First, his money is still her money, and second, sharing or giving money during this time adds insult to injury—you're already sacrificing enough by dating a man who hasn't ended his marriage yet. Don't become his rescuer, too.

Keep your things at your place. Avoid keeping any of your personal things at his home, car, office, or anywhere his ex may visit or have a key to. I know several women who have left clothing at their divorcing boyfriend's home, only to have his ex find it and create a scene, or left things in his car and had his ex search the car and steal them. Who wants to feel like a guest on Jerry Springer? Protect yourself—don't wait for him to think of it. Men *always* underestimate the wrath of a jealous woman.

Rule 4: Stay on the Periphery of His Divorce

If your relationship with a divorcing man evolves, you will become more invested in him, which puts you at risk of becoming invested in his divorce. All of a sudden, his divorce begins to feel like *your* problem. How much custody he gets, whether he gets the house, and how much maintenance he will pay his ex become things of great interest to you because they will directly impact your future with him. The problem? You have *no* power in this situation. These decisions are between him, his ex, and any lawyers, judges, and court psychologists who are involved.

Therefore, to maintain your own sense of happiness, you need to distance yourself from his divorce by following these guidelines:

Accept that it's not your money or your kid. If you become part of his life, and his kids' lives, you will feel invested in the outcome of his divorce. This is one of the quandaries of dating divorcing men—you naturally feel protective, but too much of that will backfire. He is still tying up loose ends from his married life, a life that did not involve you. This isn't your battle to fight—let him handle it.

Don't strategize or go to court with him. Again, let him handle his divorce. Being there will only make you feel anxious and powerless—and you *are* powerless. Wait for the end result. Occasionally, if you feel he could benefit from your point of view, ask him if he wants it, give it briefly and kindly, then let it go.

Don't let him lean on you too much. Divorce is one of the most stressful life events that can happen to a person. He may seek solace in you by complaining to you, asking your advice, or reporting the latest news in the soap opera of his divorce. However, burdening you with his divorce drama is unfair and selfish—you are already burdened with it simply by being with him. You want to be supportive of him without getting sucked in or turning your time together into divorce discussions. If his divorce begins to make you angry, irritable, or stressed out, it's time for him to censor himself. Tell him how it makes you feel, and tell him when you would prefer not to discuss the subject. Encourage him to vent to his friends or family.

ʃ❧ When dating Janine, Lars kept his divorce on the periphery of their relationship. Lars occasionally told Janine important information in order to keep her abreast of progress, but he made a conscious effort to handle his divorce on his own time in order to not strain the relationship. Lars, who was grateful that Janine was willing to stay with him in spite of his marital status, focused on making Janine happy. As a result, their relationship had little trouble weathering his divorce.

Rule 5: Avoid Competing with the Ex

Chapters 8 and 9 will cover dealing with exes in general; however, the ex issue is a little different when dating a divorcing man. Why? Unclear boundaries: he is with you, but still legally married to her, which often creates "competition" because both of you have certain "rights" with him. If the divorce escalates, and she is angry and trying to take his kids or money from him, you will begin to see her as the enemy. There is only one solution to this quandary: don't compete. This is *his* divorce, and it is his responsibility to compete with her, not yours. You cannot win this competition, but you can lose if you participate. Here are some guidelines for avoiding competition.

When she's the problem. If his ex resents you, it means that she is hurting. However, to avoid being on the receiving end of her pain, keep your distance from her. If she competes with you in nastier ways (she badmouths you, makes sexual overtures to him, or threatens legal revenge upon him for seeing you), step aside and let her behave childishly. If he is worth keeping, he will stand by you, reject her advances, and address her vengeful behavior in court.

When you're the problem. If you're the one feeling competitive, it's time to distance yourself. Stay on the periphery of his divorce and avoid discussing his ex with him. Talk over your feelings with friends or a therapist. And remember: assuming this man is worth being with (and he'd better be!), you've already "won" because he's with *you*.

When he's the problem. If his ex comes on to him, calls him all the time, or otherwise won't go away, don't blame her. The real problem is actually him—he needs to establish firm boundaries with his ex and refuse her advances, ignore her calls, and otherwise "cut the cord." Confront him—if he resists, the only way to avoid this unwinnable competition is to dump him. If he wants you back, he will go ahead and make the changes. Remember: the goal here is to be happy, not just keep the relationship.

Rule 6: Accept the Limitations of the Relationship

A relationship with a divorcing man means a relationship that is limited, at least until his divorce ends. If you approach the relationship as you would any other, you may wind up feeling resentful and unhappy that things aren't "normal." These are natural feelings, but you don't want them to damage your happiness or your relationship. Talk with your partner about your feelings, making sure he knows that you don't blame him. Chances are he feels the same way you do. If you focus on the bond between the two of you, you can manage the temporary limitations. However, the only limitations you should accept are the ones discussed in this chapter, which are inescapable during divorce. You should not tolerate him:

- Regularly breaking dates with you because something came up with his ex or kids
- Blowing off your birthday or other important events
- Using divorce stress as an excuse for rude or uncaring behavior
- Taking you for granted in any way

Ask for What You Want

If you review every problem in this chapter, you will see several that you have little or no control over, such as divorce delays, divorce conflict, and his legal ties to his ex. That's what work, friends, and therapists are for. However, you do have some control over a few of the other problems, such as when your partner allows his ex to manipulate him, when he talks too much about his divorce, or when he is otherwise doing something he could change. A wonderful, and crucial, skill is to be able to identify what you want or need, and then ask for it. This can be much harder than it sounds—you may feel bad putting demands on your divorcing man because he is already under pressure. You risk that he will think you are petty or high-maintenance—or worse, that he will agree with what you're saying and then do nothing to change. Then what?

Remember: a man who cares about you will want to make you happy. If he can't accommodate you, then you won't be happy in the relationship.

Is He Worth It?

One of the most difficult decisions you can face when dating a divorcing man is knowing when to cut your losses. Because of the pitfalls discussed in this chapter, some dating experts will warn you to stay away from all divorcing men. While this is extreme, perhaps you should consider only getting involved with a divorcing man if he's very special. Why? That's the only way to keep the Output (what you're getting out of the relationship) greater than the Input (what you have to give up to be in the relationship). In other words, the divorcing man has to be fabulous enough to off-set any grief you get for dating him.

The following table offers a quick way to evaluate whether he's worth it:

Keep Him	Lose Him
He's indifferent about his ex and former marriage.	He feels angry, guilty, or sad about his ex and former marriage.
He wants to be with you and makes time for you.	He seems ambivalent or preoccupied, or he breaks dates.
He answers your questions about his divorce.	He evades questions or gets angry when you want to know what's happening.
When you discuss his problems, he listens to your point of view.	He gets defensive when you express your point of view.
He accepts and supports your need for space from his divorce and to have your own life.	He gets angry or upset when you need space or doesn't understand how difficult his divorce is for you.
He takes responsibility for dealing with his divorce.	He blames the ex/lawyers/judge for the difficulties in his divorce.
He focuses on his relationship with you and tries to meet your needs during his divorce.	He focuses on his divorce and is primarily concerned with getting his own needs met.
He has scheduled time with his children, and shows strong boundaries with his ex.	He interrupts plans to deal with everyday issues with his kids or ex or allows his ex to manipulate him.
You feel happy with him most of the time, even if you are unhappy with his divorcing status.	In addition to his divorcing status, you feel unhappy with him or your relationship on a regular basis.

Dating a divorcing man requires a lot of patience, a high tolerance for stress and discomfort, and a solid sense of self. The sooner you can spot problems, the sooner you can fix them, or get out without investing too much. Fortunately, this type of relationship can succeed with the right man.

To truly succeed, you must *be happy together,* not simply stay together. Some women who have dated divorcing men have witnessed unremarkable divorces, while others saw terrible ones. No one has ever been thrilled about dating a divorcing man, but if you've found a great guy and can see it through, you'll be glad you did.

SIX

A Man with a Past:
The Divorced Man

Finally! A man who isn't married, putting off filing for divorce, or slogging through his divorce. If you've met a man who can actually show you proof of his divorce decree, you're already several steps ahead. Of course, this doesn't mean that you have nothing to worry about—divorced men still have plenty of challenges to keep you on your toes. If your relationship works out long-term, some of the following challenges in this chapter have important implications for your future.

The Divorced Man

So, if divorced men are legally free from their former marriages, what makes them different from other single men who've had serious relationships but never been married? Divorced men are different because the end of a marriage often leaves remnants, or *baggage*, that one doesn't usually see from a nonmarital relationship. Some of these remnants are permanent, such as children. Others are just stubborn, like emotional consequences, financial difficulties, and problematic ex-wives. These remnants can be challenging for you because they're constant reminders of his past, and because you often have limited control over them.

In addition, compared to a nonmarital breakup, divorce often leads to greater levels of loss for everyone involved. These feelings of loss differ from divorce to divorce, but here are some of the more common feelings.

Loss of the "Until Death Do You Part" Ideal

People marry with the goal of staying together forever. Thus, the end of a marriage triggers feelings not only of loss for the relationship, but also of loss of the ideal that things would work out long-term. In some divorced men, this can engender a sense of failure or a loss of faith in marriage and long-term commitment, possibly resulting in hesitancy at making such a commitment in the future.

Loss of Relationships

When two people marry, many bonds form. And when divorce occurs, many of those bonds are broken or changed. A divorced man must contend with changes in relationships with his ex, her family, and any "couple friends" they had.

Loss of Property

Married couples buy things together, and create a home together. Thus, when divorce occurs, they must divide everything between them. Important things like houses, pets, and other things of sentimental value can't be split in half, and can only go to one person.

Loss of Time with Children

Before divorce, both parents live in the same place with the kids, and therefore have complete access to them. After divorce, the kids are either at Mom's or Dad's, reducing the amount of time each parent sees the kids. Dads typically have even less time with their children than moms do.

Thus, the divorced man typically has more "baggage" than a never-married guy. Fortunately, not all baggage is permanent, and not all baggage is necessarily bad. For you, the trick is to figure out how much baggage he has, and whether any of that baggage is a problem for you.

Not all divorced men are the same: there's a big difference between a recently divorced man with three young children and a huge child-support payment and a man with no children who's been divorced for years. As a general rule, the first man will come with many more challenges and difficulties than the second one. For example, while writing this chapter, I had dinner with a married couple I am friends with. They've been married for three years, and I've known the husband for ten years. When I mentioned this chapter, the wife said I should talk with her about the subject. "I didn't know you'd dated a divorced man," I said to her. "I married one!" she said, pointing to her partner. Although I've known this man for a decade, I'd actually forgotten that he had been married before. Because the marriage ended more than ten years ago, and produced no children, there were no real remnants of his former marriage in his current life. Thus, there is little difference between my friend, who has a low Difficulty Index, and a guy who's never been married.

This section covers the five main problems with divorced men, and the next chapter discusses the five rules for dating divorced men.

The Five Problems with Divorced Men

The following problems do not apply to every divorced man, and the extent of these problems will vary:

1. He's still living in the past.
2. He hasn't learned from his mistakes.
3. He isn't interested in remarrying or having children.
4. He has financial obligations.
5. You're not his top priority.

Problem 1: He's Still Living in the Past

One thing that makes divorce so difficult for people is that it involves so many changes. Change can be difficult, especially for some types of people. When a man gets divorced, the period between physical separation and the final divorce date helps him adjust to some of the changes. However, depending on the circumstances—and the man—the adjustment period can last longer, even well beyond the divorce. Thus, when people have difficulty adjusting to change, they cling to what's familiar—in this case, the marriage, the ex, and the past. The important thing is to differentiate between a man experiencing the normal adjustments that divorce requires and a man who has not let go of his married life. Look out for the following signs that he may still be living in the past:

Pining over the past. Some men have a difficult time letting go of their marriages. Some have regrets, and wish they could go back in time and fix their mistakes. Others glorify the past, remembering only the good things about the ex or the marriage, and forgetting the bad. In fact, polls have shown that after divorcing, men are much more likely than women to wish they could give it another go with their ex.

🕊 John and his ex, who had one child together, got divorced after five years of marriage. Although John and his ex did not have a good marriage, and his ex had no desire to be with him, for years afterward John wished he could reunite with his ex. He liked the idea of a nuclear family, and wanted his child to live with both parents. When he began dating Angela, the relationship never really went anywhere, and he finally admitted his wishes to Angela. They stopped seeing each other. John eventually realized that getting back with his ex would never happen, and he moved on with someone else.

Nonessential contact with his ex. This type of contact includes regular phone calls, helping his ex with home repairs, going over to his old house to see the kids (instead of picking them up), and spending birthdays and holidays with his ex or his ex and kids, as if they were still a family. This does not include contact to deal with issues regarding the children. However, the occasional nonessential friendly lunch or phone call is okay. If he hasn't started dating, this sort of behavior isn't problematic—but once you two become serious, it's inappropriate. It tells you that he has a family already, and you aren't a part of it.

🕊 Susan met Darren in a local cycling club, and has been dating him for six months. Darren had been divorced for five months before he began dating Susan, and has no children. During the first few months with Darren, Susan began to see that while Darren was divorced, his ex still played a prominent role in his life. For example, Darren's ex would call his cell phone while Susan and Darren were having dinner together, and he would take the calls. Darren's ex often asked him to fix things at her place, and he obliged her. Finally, Darren admitted to Susan that he and his ex would be participating in the same cycling race, and were planning to go to the race together.

Clearly, Darren hasn't let go of his past yet, and Susan isn't going to get much out of her relationship with him because the ex is still a dominant factor in his life. This example illustrates the importance of boundaries—because Darren does not have firm boundaries with his ex, his relationship with Susan includes a third party.

Talking about the past. A man who is still living in the past will talk about his past often. This can include:

* Talking about his ex, whether good or bad things
* Talking about his marriage, and what was good or bad about it
* Referring to the past too often (for example, you go to a football game, and he refers back to football games he went to with his ex)

WHY DOES HE CLING TO THE PAST?

He never wanted the divorce. A man whose divorce was forced upon him may have the hardest time letting go of the past. He believed the marriage could work and that the divorce should never have happened. Thus, until he accepts that there was a good reason his marriage ended, he will always live in the past. Any woman who gets involved with him before this acceptance will take second place to his ex-wife and former marriage.

He has regrets. When their marriages fall apart, some men struggle for a long time over their part in it. If he worked too much, or cheated on his ex, he may realize that it contributed to the divorce. Other men may not have done anything that so obviously contributed to the divorce, but still feel frustrated that they were not able to fix the problems and keep the marriage together. Although that sounds more like something a woman would do, the fact is that men pride themselves on being able to "handle" things. A divorce can feel like a "failure" and lead to feelings of regret.

He's recently divorced. At this time, he is still adjusting to his new life and may have some old habits to break. Even though he probably made many adjustments during his separation, a divorce is a stressful period of transition. Once it is over, he can settle into a routine that doesn't involve haggling with his ex.

He's slow to change. Some men take longer than others to deal with change. These men prefer the familiar over the novel. Even if his former marriage wasn't so great, it was familiar, and thus represents a sort of comfort to him.

Steer clear of a man who is still stuck in the past. He needs some time to put the past behind him, and you're better off giving him that time before you date him. Dating a man who's stuck in the past is dating a man who isn't really available—you shouldn't have to settle for that.

Problem 2: He Hasn't Learned from His Mistakes

You've probably heard the saying "Those who forget history are doomed to repeat it." In relationship terms, this means that a man who doesn't learn what went wrong in his former marriage is likely to repeat the same mistakes with you. Of course, figuring out what went wrong in his marriage is trickier that it seems. When asked what ended their marriages, people will often cite the *symptoms* (we fought a lot, we fell out of love) or the straw that broke the camel's back (she cheated on me) rather than the *cause*. At first glance, you can understand how fighting or cheating could lead to divorce. However, fighting and cheating are symptoms of basic incompatibility or serious flaws in one or both partners.

"Why is this important?" you ask. "Can't he just let the past be the past and move forward?" Yes, but only if he's *learned* from his past. If he hasn't, it will come to haunt him (and you) in the present. This issue is especially important for remarriage, and is one reason why stepfamilies experience difficulty. Is it any wonder that the divorce rate for second marriages is higher than for first marriages?

It boils down to this: has he figured out what led to his divorce, and has he made changes to prevent making those mistakes again? Here are some signs that he hasn't learned from his mistakes.

He has no clue what caused his divorce. When asked why their marriages didn't work out, some men will toss out a canned reason such as "We fought all the time." Again, you can understand why a couple who fights all the time might wind up divorced, but fighting is a symptom of marital discord, not a cause. He should have asked himself, "What did we fight about? Did we fight because we were highly incompatible, because one of us drank too much, or because we were overwhelmed with the responsibilities of two jobs and three children?" True, not everybody is sophisticated when it comes to understanding the intricacies of marital problems. However, anyone can talk with a therapist, talk with friends, read a book on breakups, or otherwise figure out a way to get some insight into what went wrong and how to avoid the same mistakes in the future.

He blames his ex. If you ask a man why he got divorced and he replies, "She cheated on me" or "She left me," he is not off the hook. If she cheated, this man should be asking himself, "Why did she cheat? Was I working too much and neglecting her? Was I loving and supportive enough to her? Did she have a history of infidelity that I chose to ignore when I married her?" Even if he was a caring husband and she a long-time cheat, he needs to understand his role in the problems. Whatever the cause was, he must claim some responsibility and learn from his mistakes. Blaming his ex only turns him into a victim, and prevents him from learning from his mistakes.

You're similar to his ex. Okay, so you're a tall brunette and so is she. Is that a problem? Probably not. However, over time, you may find that you have similar qualities as hers; in particular, you and she may have the same qualities that created friction for him and her. For example, he's a passive guy who hated his ex-wife's bossiness. You're a take-charge gal. If you find yourself wanting to boss him around, look out.

He's eager to remarry. Considering how gun-shy a divorce can make a man, you may have a positive reaction to his eagerness to try again. However, a willingness to remarry is good, but an eagerness to do so can be a red flag. This is especially true for recently divorced men (i.e., the divorce finalized less than a year ago), but keep a wary eye out for any divorced man who is eager to remarry. Why? Too much eagerness means he liked married life, dislikes single life, and is looking to fill the void. Research has shown that married men, more than married women, fare much better than single ones in terms of mental and physical health. If you're eager as well, you both may make an unwise choice in marriage.

Overall, if you sense that he doesn't seem to know what went wrong in his marriage, probe him about it. He may just not want to give you the gory details or admit his part in it because he fears it will make him look bad. Encourage him to talk about it by telling him that you would expect that he made mistakes. Hopefully he'll show some insight and some willingness to take responsibility. If he doesn't, take a walk. Otherwise, his next divorce could be with you.

Problem 3: He Isn't Interested in Remarrying or Having Children

It isn't uncommon to hear a divorcing or divorced man claim that he's had it with women and that marriage sucks. This is a normal part of grieving a broken marriage. However, most men will recover from this stage—no matter how tough they act, men are suckers for love, just like women. And census statistics don't lie: the vast majority of divorced men remarry within a few years of their divorces. However, there are several factors that can influence his desire for remarriage or children:

He was rejected or cheated on. These events can really devastate a man, enough to make him want to avoid opening his heart. Being cheated on can be especially damaging to a man's sense of strength or "manhood." However, the pain of these events does not have to be long-term.

Like all other relationship disasters, they can be faced, dealt with, learned from, and healed. And only after he goes through this process will he be a good partner.

His divorce was contentious or financially devastating to him. When a man gets his clock cleaned in his divorce, he isn't eager to marry again. This is also why many men become fans of the prenuptial agreement. Can you blame him? However, as with being rejected or cheated on, he can choose to learn from the past, and heal.

He has children. A man who has children will probably want to remarry, but he may or may not want more children. Not only are children a tremendous responsibility; they require financial resources. His child support obligations never change, even if he has five kids with you. He may feel overwhelmed by these responsibilities, and feel that another child is too much. Or, he may simply state that he's "done" with having kids.

Art is a thirty-nine-year-old divorced man with two teenaged daughters who live with him half of the time. Although he is willing to remarry, he stated that he will not get involved with women who want children. He feels that the responsibility of having two kids is more than enough, and cannot fathom the idea of starting over and investing eighteen more years in raising another child.

He's older. Once men get past the usual family-starting years (beyond age forty-five or so), their interest in marriage and children may wane. Often, men who are this age and older have children who are fully grown, and the idea of starting all over again seems crazy to them. So, you may be thirty-eight and interested in having children, and dating a forty-five-year-old man who has a kid in college! However, this is only a guideline—every man is different, and men don't have biological clocks.

Because marriage and children are such important issues, don't waste too much time before finding out what his feelings are on this subject. If you want marriage or children and he does not, that constitutes a deal-breaker. Never settle on these issues in order to be with him, and don't stick around while hoping he will change his mind. Settling on such crucial issues will only wear down your relationship, and prolong your getting what you want. And because of the biological clock issue, you don't want to waste time waiting for him to change his mind.

An important side note: Some men will state a preference for no children, but say they are willing to have them with you if you want them. This is a "deal-maker," and his way of showing you that he will compromise because he wants to be with you. However, there are risks—a man who in his heart doesn't want children may grow to resent having one with you, and he may not turn out to be the best father. This may wear down your relationship in the long run. Therefore, take great care in deciding what you want in this situation.

Problem 4: He Has Financial Obligations

One of the most concrete realities of divorce is how financially devastating it can be. The divorced man can have many financial burdens to contend with, including:

- Divorce-related debts, including lawyers' fees and custody evaluation fees
- Other debts left over from the marriage or divorce
- Child support and/or spousal maintenance payments
- Credit problems from the marriage or divorce

Thus, the divorced man may be strapped for cash even if he earns a good income. How strapped he is depends on several factors, but as a rule, the largest cash-eaters are children and an ex-wife who didn't work during their marriage. In these situations, he will have to pay child support and other child-related expenses, and he will probably pay maintenance (alimony) to his ex. Debts and credit problems are less immediately taxing on the wallet, but can have more serious implications.

Why are his finances important? Money matters influence the types of activities you can do together. The more financially constrained he is, the simpler your dates and activities will be. But more importantly, his financial obligations become a bigger issue if your relationship becomes serious. If you move in together or marry, you may find yourselves struggling to pay bills or buy a house; in order to get by, or meet goals, your income may have to compensate for his monthly payments toward debts, child support, and alimony. The more serious his financial situation, the more at risk you are for becoming resentful—after all, it's frustrating to find your life being constrained by financial problems you had no part in creating. This is especially true when his ex-wife doesn't work or spends the money on expensive shoes. These annoyances can put stress on your relationship. Chapter 14 discusses these financial issues in greater detail.

For dating purposes, just be aware that a divorced man may have financial struggles. Fortunately, many divorce-related financial problems are temporary. With planning, you both can work around these issues.

Problem 5: You're Not His Top Priority

If you're dating a divorced man, when it comes to his time, attention, and effort, you may find yourself in line behind a number of people. These people usually include his children and his ex-wife. He may have other worries that preoccupy him, including the responsibilities of parenting, or his finances. You may find it difficult to know where you should stand in this situation. Thus, here are some guidelines:

- When you first begin dating him, give him a chance to make room for you in his life. Try not to spend too much time with him or make demands. However, he should always respect you and your time—don't tolerate lateness, missed phone calls, or cancelled dates, unless very rare and accompanied by an apology.
- After dating for a while, once things move toward a relationship, you should begin to take priority over his ex. For example, he should not take her calls when spending time with you. However, his children's needs and activities will come first, and you will have to work around those.
- Over time, his ex should take less and less priority. He shouldn't be fixing her car or acting as her confidante. It's okay if they remain friends, but their friendship should involve the occasional chat or lunch, and should be scheduled around your time with him.
- Eventually, if you and he move in together or marry, you should generally attain the same priority as his children. In some situations, they'll have priority. In others, you will. This issue is discussed further in Chapter 16. Some people, including some "experts," will tell you to accept that you will always come second to his children. Early on, his children will come first. But after you make a serious commitment, this is unacceptable.

In summary, the divorced man can come with his own set of challenges. The next chapter will provide some tips on how to deal with these challenges.

SEVEN

The Five Rules for Dating Divorced Men

Now that you're acquainted with the problems that come with divorced men, here are several guidelines to follow when dating these men:

1. Ask plenty of questions as soon as possible.
2. Assess his baggage.
3. Take things slowly.
4. Evaluate your needs.
5. Be adaptable.

Rule 1: Ask Plenty of Questions as Soon as Possible

Just as previous chapters advised, it is imperative that you ask the divorced man plenty of questions, as early as possible. Since asking personal questions is never easy, be sure to see Chapter 3 for advice on how to ask questions. Here are some questions you may want to ask a divorced man:

When his divorce was finalized. Ask this question as soon as you can. His answer will tell you two things: whether he's divorced yet, and if so, how long he's been divorced. Be sure to phrase it with the word "finalized" in there somewhere; otherwise, since the word "divorced" can mean "separated" or "getting divorced" to some men, you may not get the whole truth. As you know, a man who is still in the process of divorce is a whole different animal, and a greater risk (see Chapter 4). Also, the longer he's been divorced, the better, as that usually means fewer emotional hang-ups for him, fewer financial issues, and fewer problems with the ex-wife, children, and family.

Whether he has children. This is another question to ask as soon as you can. Why waste your time going out with a man who has children if you don't want to date a man with children? Also, you will have a much better idea of what to expect from him if you know he has the responsibilities of children.

How much he has his children. If you don't mind that he has children, find out how much he has them. A man with 40 percent or more time with his kids is more involved and won't have the freedom that a father with less parenting time might have. A man with the more traditional every-other-weekend model, or something similar amounting to under 40 percent, has greater availability and is more likely to allow Mom to take on more of the parenting responsibilities.

The type of relationship he has with his ex. You may get a neutral answer to this question in the beginning, but you should observe over time how he talks about her. The worse their relationship, the sooner you'll know about it. Ideally, she is out of his life. This isn't possible if they have children together; in this case, the better they get along, the easier things will be for him, and you. If they remained friends, that can be good or bad.

Does he want to remarry eventually? Does he want more children? To avoid making him nervous, wait until you feel pretty comfortable around each other before asking these questions. Also, ask these questions generically, as part of simply getting to know him. He'll know you're feeling him out, but if you wait until he's comfortable with you, and you aren't trying to rush the relationship, he probably won't mind answering them. Once he does, believe his answers. Unless he's newly divorced, he probably won't change his mind.

Rule 2: Assess His Baggage

When you date a divorced man, his baggage may be manageable or unmanageable, but if you know how much there is in advance, you can plan ahead for how to deal with it. Thus, when you get involved with a divorced man, you will need to do a baggage assessment.

To do this, examine the list on the following page—for each row, circle the item from Column 1, 2, or 3 that best describes his situation.

Baggage Assessment for Divorced Men (circle all that apply)			
	Column 1	*Column 2*	*Column 3*
Number of children	No children	One child	Two or more children
Parenting time	Once in a while, or summers only	Every other weekend	40 percent or more of the time
Children's ages	17 and up	7–16	6 and under
Children's behavior	Polite and well-adjusted	Distant or slow to warm up	Rude, bratty, or poorly behaved
Maintenance payments	None	Small or short in duration	Large or long in duration
Financial problems	None	Some debts from marriage	Large debts or credit problems from marriage
Ex-wife	Polite or absent	Annoying or overinvolved	Angry/Difficult
Attitude about former marriage	Glad it's over, or understands why it ended	Somewhat clueless about why marriage ended	Bitter, has no clue why it ended, or refuses to talk about it
Attitude/ treatment toward his ex	Polite or indifferent	Annoyance or avoidance	Angry, disrespectful, or guilty

Once you have circled your answers, examine which column has the greatest number of circles.

If your circles are primarily in Column 1, he has little to no baggage. If most of your circles are in Column 2, he has a moderate level of baggage. If most of your circles are in Column 3, you are dating a man with high levels of baggage.

If your circles spread across more than one column, take the average. For example, if half your circles are in Column 1 and half are in Column 2, then he has mild to moderate baggage.

Overall, moderate baggage is doable, as long as any problems improve with time. For example, problems like an angry ex-wife and children who are slow to warm up need to improve before you move in with or marry him. Other things, like children and debt, simply require some planning, and making sure your Output is high enough. A high-baggage situation with too many circles in Column 3 is too overwhelming, and getting involved with a man in this situation is generally not a good idea. However, no matter what his baggage situation is, make sure your Output is greater than your Input.

Rule 3: Take Things Slowly

As you have probably noticed, these three words appear many times throughout this book. With a divorced man, you don't have to be as concerned about going slowly as you would with a separated or divorcing man. However, as illustrated in the "Five Problems with Divorced Men" in Chapter 6, divorced men can come with problems, too. Your goal is to detect these problems before you get seriously involved with him, and that takes time. In addition, once you assess how much baggage he has, that will guide you in just how slow to take things. The greater the baggage, the slower you should go.

Unfortunately, when a woman proceeds too quickly in a relationship with a divorced man, she winds up falling for him before she knows everything she needs to know about him. Then she is at much greater risk for compromising her needs in order to keep the relationship.

♫ When single Renee met divorced man Brian, the chemistry between them was very palpable. They had a lot in common and fell in love quickly. Renee thought she'd met the man for her.

However, after spending more time with Brian, she found out he had a considerable amount of baggage: an angry and demanding ex-wife, whom he catered to, and significant financial problems. Renee was taken aback at Brian's baggage, but loved him so much that she was willing to overlook it. Two years later, after having moved in with Brian and fully faced his mean ex and the realities of his finances, Renee finally left him, broken-hearted that everything had fallen apart.

❧ When Marie began dating divorced man Joel, they were both conscious of the need to take things slowly. They waited a couple of months to get sexually involved, and Marie focused on getting to know Joel before complicating matters by meeting his son and daughter. Things were going very well until Joel began to show signs that he hadn't learned from his past mistakes with his ex—his ex had wanted the divorce, and she'd quickly gotten involved with another man, but Joel never really understood what had gone wrong. He began showing signs of withdrawal and moodiness with Marie once their relationship became more serious. Soon after, they stopped seeing each other. Marie was disappointed that things didn't work out, but quickly moved on with her life.

These examples illustrate why going slowly is important. Renee and Brian moved too quickly, making it much more difficult for Renee to deal objectively with some potentially serious problems—if they had slowed things down, Renee could have asked Brian to deal with his ex and financial problems before investing more of herself, or left the relationship before she invested two years of her life. On the other hand, Marie took things more slowly—she got to know Joel before getting too emotionally involved or meeting his children. Even though her relationship with Joel ended, she invested less of herself, wasted less time, and experienced less pain when things didn't work out. In some cases, going slowly can even save the relationship by allowing any fixable problems to work themselves out.

Here are some ways you should take things slowly with a divorced man:

- Don't see him too often or rush into a relationship with him until you have a good idea of what his situation is like. Then, if he has more problems than you bargained for, you can choose to keep going slowly, or leave the relationship.
- If he has children, wait until you and he become somewhat serious before meeting them. Then you'll be a potentially permanent person in their lives, rather than one of a string of women Dad's dated. However, don't wait too long—you don't want to get too attached to him before you have a chance to assess his children.
- When you choose to get sexually involved with him is your choice, but waiting months, and not weeks, may help to keep the relationship from moving too quickly on an emotional level.
- Don't move in together, and never marry, until you've read this entire book and have found out and experienced his entire kid, ex, family, and financial situation. If there are problems, you should know what they are *before* you choose to commit to him—thus, you make an informed decision.

Rule 4: Evaluate Your Needs

One of the tricky things about dating divorced men, especially men with children, is that your needs can get swallowed up by the demands of his situation. You may feel that you don't want to impose too much on this man because you can see he's already loaded up with his own problems. You may try to ask little from him, and blend into his life rather than add to his list of burdens. Although this is very thoughtful of you, it is a mistake. Whether you know it or not, you have needs. Trying to sacrifice or compromise any of them will only lead to unhappiness down the road. Besides, if he finds that you don't ask for much, he'll learn that he doesn't have to give much. Not a good way to start a relationship.

You may say, "Wait a minute. If I need lots of attention from him, but he has kids that need his attention also, don't his kids' needs come first?" This isn't about whose needs come first—this is about figuring out whether this relationship can meet your needs. If it can, great. If it can't, then it *will not work* over the long haul. Thus, it is extremely important that you figure out what you need in a relationship.

Here are some difficult questions you need to ask yourself when you get involved in a relationship with a divorced man. You probably won't know the answers to these questions until you've spent some quality time together, but keep them in mind:

- Am I comfortable sharing the man in my life with his children?
- Am I comfortable having my life influenced by children's needs?
- Am I comfortable with how this man raises his children?
- Am I comfortable with a man who must, because of children, deal with his ex-wife on a regular basis?
- Am I comfortable being with a man who has a relationship with his ex-wife, has lunch with her, or fixes things at her home?
- Do I get enough time, love, and support from this man?
- Does this man treat me and my time with respect?
- Am I a high enough priority in this man's life?

- Am I comfortable with this man's debts, or the fact that he pays his ex-wife a large sum of money each month?
- Anything else you can think of that's important to you, *no matter how small.*

You may not know you have some of these needs until you date a man who doesn't quite meet them. That's okay— one of the goals of dating is to figure out what you really need in a relationship. That's why I encourage you to take things slowly, and always be honest with yourself about what you need. If he can't meet your needs, you will find someone who does.

Rule 5: Be Adaptable

Once you determine what your needs are and feel that they are being met, you may still find that there are some things you can't change or control when you date a divorced man. Part of the challenge of dating or having a relationship with a divorced man is becoming accustomed to his divorce-related baggage. Unless he is baggage-free, this process takes time. The lifestyle that comes with children probably requires the greatest amount of adaptability. However, while adapting is good (and necessary if you want to be happy with him), just make sure that you adapt *after* you've evaluated your needs and are certain they are being met.

This is a multistage process: early on, you will have certain basic needs (for example, that he calls when he says he will call). If you feel these basic needs are met, you can begin, for example, adapting to the fact that he's been married before. Over time, your needs will increase, you will re-evaluate whether they're being met, and you will adapt accordingly. *Never* try to adapt to a situation that doesn't meet your needs—it will only create unhappiness.

Despite the problems that can come with divorced men, these men are generally a very eligible group. Too much baggage is no good, but once a man has grieved his marriage and gotten his baggage to a manageable level, he's in good shape. Many women have married wonderful divorced men—which means that there are more out there like them.

EIGHT

The Other Woman: The Ex

One day, I was talking with Greg, a male colleague of mine, about a married couple I know: a woman married to a divorced man. When I mentioned that the divorced man's ex-wife was "bad news," Greg looked at me with some surprise and said, "Aren't all ex-wives bad news?" Like many others, Greg associates the word "ex-wife" with something negative. Unfortunately, this stereotype has some truth to it—some women simply aren't skilled at handling their ex-husbands, or their ex-husbands' new girlfriends. But, fortunately, many ex-wives aren't a problem at all. The difficult thing is that you may not see ex-related problems until you become a more integral part of his life—e.g., when you move in together or marry. However, if you pay close attention, you can get a pretty good idea of what she's like while you and he are still in the dating period.

Figuring Out the Ex

Generally speaking, his ex-wife will typically fall into one of the following three categories:

The Polite or Absent Ex-wife: A Polite or Absent Ex-wife is friendly and kind, or polite and distant, or totally absent. If they have children together, she is able to co-parent with him without much conflict. Your relationship with her consists of a polite exchange now and again, or there is no relationship with her at all. This woman has adjusted to the divorce and has a life of her own.

The Ever-Present Ex-wife: The Ever-Present Ex is the type of ex you wish would go away. She calls too often, she needs help with one thing or another, she's always having a crisis, or she's overly concerned about what the kids do when they're with him. This woman hasn't adjusted to life after divorce, and she may not be over him yet.

The Angry/Difficult Ex-wife: Not surprisingly, the Angry/Difficult Ex is the worst type of ex. She is rude, angry, or jealous, she badmouths you and your partner to others (including any children), or she tries to keep him from seeing his kids. In extreme cases, she is capable of illegal activity such as harassment, theft, or vandalism. This woman definitely has not adjusted to her divorce. She is typically psychologically unhealthy, and has difficulty in other areas of her life.

Why is it important to categorize ex-wives like this? Because which category she fits in will predict not only how difficult she is to deal with but also how difficult your life may be if you get involved with her ex-husband. Obviously, a Polite or Absent Ex-wife is the best type of ex, as she will not cause much trouble, if any. Ever-Present and Angry/Difficult Ex-wives tend to create problems, both for him and you, which can create strain on your relationship. For example, you and he may differ on how to deal with her. If she's an Angry/

Difficult Ex, he may spend a lot of time in court battles, or both of you may experience numerous visits to attorneys or the police. However, as you will see in this chapter, a bad ex is not a deal-breaker *if* certain rules and guidelines are followed.

It is important to mention that during divorce, or after a recent divorce, a limited amount of "ever-presence" or mild difficulty with the ex is normal, particularly if they have children. She may be in turmoil, or accustomed to being the primary caretaker and adjusting to the new parenting time arrangement. This behavior should resolve with time.

Once you determine whether his ex is Polite or Absent, Ever-Present, or Angry/Difficult, the second thing you need to determine is how much his ex "factors" into his life: how much contact he has with her, and how much power she has in his life. This is important because the more she factors into his life, the more she'll factor into your life. There are five main issues that determine how much the ex factors in.

His Marital Status

With a divorced man, the ex may or may not be in the picture. However, if he's still separated or getting divorced, she factors in a great deal, and has power due to the fact that they are still legally married. In this case, she still has legal control over their money, home, cars, and other property. There's a good chance she has some emotional pull as well. However, his marital status will eventually change.

Children

If they have children together, his ex-wife factors into his life a great deal, and will factor in permanently. The ex is not only "around," but she has power because of parental rights. However, she can still fall under any one of the three categories:

How Long They've Been Apart

The longer he and his ex have been split up, the greater the chance that she is over him and has moved on. If they don't have children together, she probably won't be in the picture at all after a while. If they do have children, they should have worked out some of the "kinks" in their co-parenting relationship over time.

Who Initiated the Divorce

If she initiated the divorce, she will factor into his life less because she's more likely to be over him and ready to move on. One woman I interviewed has dated five divorced men, and she never had a problem with any of the ex-wives. It turns out these five men had one thing in common: their wives wanted the divorce. If she's over him, she's rarely a problem.

If She Has a New Partner

A new partner typically means she is over her ex and is receiving support from another man. Most troublesome exes don't have new partners, and may factor into his life because they are looking for support or feeling resentful that he has moved on. Of course, there are exceptions—some women remarry and still behave inappropriately.

You can combine all the above information to get a good idea of what you may be dealing with when you get involved with him. For example:

- A Polite or Absent Ex-wife and no children =
  You will probably never meet her.
- An Ever-Present Ex-wife he's still divorcing =
  She will probably call him a lot.

- An Angry/Difficult Ex-wife with no boyfriend, and they have children = *Beware!*

The Five Problems with Exes

Now that you understand the different types of ex-wives, this next section will cover the problems that can come with exes, and the next chapter will discuss some rules for dealing with the ex. Here are the five factors that can make an ex-wife particularly hard to deal with:

1. She isn't over him.
2. She hates you.
3. She's a permanent part of his life.
4. He mishandles her.
5. You have big shoes to fill.

Problem 1: She Isn't Over Him

Unfortunately, a separated or divorced man may be over his ex, but she may not be over him. If he left her and initiated the divorce, you can bet she isn't over him, unless the divorce was years ago. However, some women hang on to an ex-partner even if she initiated the split. His finding a new woman only increases the pain these women are in, as it means that he has moved on. So why doesn't she "move on" as well? There are a couple of reasons.

Most people think long and hard before initiating a divorce. By the time they go through with it, they are further along in the grieving process than their spouse is. Thus, when a man leaves his wife, she will lag behind him in this process.

Additionally, regardless of who initiates the divorce, some women simply have a difficult time letting go of relationships, and thus take longer to grieve. This is especially true for women who were dependent on their husbands (financially or otherwise), or who don't have much self-esteem.

EIGHT SIGNS HIS EX ISN'T OVER HIM YET

Initiating contact: She calls regularly to talk, or wants to spend time with him beyond the occasional lunch.

Affection: She touches him or tries to kiss him, even when she knows about you.

Dependence: She tells him how sad or lonely she is, seeks his advice, or asks him to help her fix her fridge, do her taxes, etc.

Desperation: She pleads with him to move back in or give their marriage another try, or makes sexual overtures to him to try to get him to sleep with her.

Anger: She's rude to him in person, on the phone, or in e-mail, and finds reasons to create conflict with him.

Indifference to you: She does not acknowledge you or greet you on the phone.

Jealousy: She makes rude or insulting remarks about you to him, or is rude and insulting to you directly.

Revenge: She tries to prevent him from seeing his children, threatens to take him to court for more money, or does anything nasty to him or you.

A grieving ex-wife can display any or all of these behaviors. If you encounter these behaviors, you may feel your own range of emotions: fear, anger, pity, disgust. The solution to this problem is up to your partner: he *must* make it crystal clear to his ex that their relationship is over, and that he will not tolerate the unacceptable behaviors. See the rules in the next chapter on how to deal with a grieving ex.

So what are the signs that his ex *is* over him? Although friendly or polite behavior is a good sign, it isn't always realistic after divorce. The true sign that she is over him is indifference—she keeps her distance and doesn't display any behavior, good or bad, that you would expect from a wife.

Problem 2: She Hates You

Unless you have done something unfriendly to her, there is only one reason a man's ex-wife will hate you: she's jealous. The roots of her jealousy come down to two things: pain and insecurity. As far as pain is concerned, a hateful ex-wife is still grieving the loss of her marriage, and is stuck in the "anger" stage of the grieving process. Instead of trying to heal her pain, she acts out, seeking to hurt the person who she perceives hurt her first (i.e., you). Feelings of insecurity can also lead to her hating you. A grieving ex may feel anger from time to time, but if she directs her anger at you, that means she's struggling with strong feelings of inadequacy.

Although pain and insecurity are the sources of an ex-wife's hatred, several things can encourage hatred in her:

He cheated on her with you. Cheating will turn even the most reasonable woman into a woman who hates you. This is one of many reasons to avoid getting involved with him until after he separates, no matter how "over" the marriage is—she may still hate you if you wait to get involved with him, but then her hatred will seem petty, and you won't feel as guilty as you would if he cheated on her with you.

He's not divorced yet. Many ex-wives simply don't like that another woman is in the picture when things aren't completely "over" yet. She will wonder if he spends their money on you, if you are around her children, or if you helped make the divorce happen. Ultimately, that's her problem. But until the divorce has been under way for many months, it's better (for your sake) to keep a low profile.

He left her to be with you. n this case, she may blame you for causing their divorce. Even if he never cheated with you, she will probably assume he did. However, it's up to him, not you, to deal with her and to provide any explanation to her. Again, try to keep a low profile for a while to spare yourself the aggravation.

Although the above factors increase the probability that she will hate you, you may find that an ex can hate you simply because you exist. Even if she left him, she may not like being replaced so quickly, or that you spend time with her children. The simple fact is, some women don't handle loss well—these women act out when dumped for another woman, and they act out when they dump a guy and he finds another woman. These women don't have a solid sense of self, and need to feel like they have control or power over a man.

So what do you do? Steer clear of her, and let her deal with her feelings. Don't talk with her, apologize to her, or otherwise try to win her over—these actions will only make things worse. Ultimately, they're *her* feelings and *she* needs to come to terms with them. Most importantly, your man needs to step in and take control—this usually has the most powerful, and lasting, effect.

Problem 3: She's a Permanent Part of His Life

Polite or Absent, Ever-Present, Angry or Difficult, there are certain situations in which an ex will remain in his life. This means that if your relationship with him works out, she will become part of *your* life. There are two primary ways an ex can remain a permanent part of a divorced man's life.

They have children together. Children guarantee that his ex is always in his life, one way or another. No matter what she's like, he's stuck with her, which means you are, too. However, being stuck with her does *not* mean you should be at the mercy of any bad behavior from her.

They're friends. Although not typical, sometimes a divorced man remains friends with his ex. The good news: if he retains a friendship with her, she's probably a decent person and won't cause problems. The bad news: under certain circumstances, their relationship can interfere with yours. Everybody has a different opinion on whether a man should stay friends with his ex. The important thing to examine is the nature of the relationship. For example:

- How often do they have contact? The greater the frequency, the more you should be concerned. The occasional friendly phone call or lunch never hurt anyone. But regular contact can indicate a deeper connection.
- What's the nature of the contact? Does she show signs of not being over him? Does he feel sorry for her or feel

guilty for leaving her? Is he always helping her? Does he seem to want or need her advice or companionship? These are not good signs, and show a relationship based on neediness, not friendliness.

𝕁𝕦 April met divorced man Tony through a mutual friend. Tony had been divorced for two years, and he'd had an amicable divorce. Tony told April right up front that he was good friends with his ex-wife and would not give up the friendship. April found that Tony and his ex kept in touch, but kept their conversations appropriate. Tony included April in occasional gatherings his ex hosted, and Tony's ex was polite and friendly to April. As a result, April had no problem with his friendship with his ex.

If he is connected to his ex besides casual, respectful friendship, or co-parenting responsibilities, you will never feel comfortable. Who wants to share her partner with his ex?

Problem 4: He Mishandles Her

When you date a separated or divorced man and encounter problems with his ex, more often than not he is a major part of the problem. Many women forget this fact. If he has an Ever-Present or Angry/Difficult ex, it's easy to see yourself as a soldier in a battle, where you and he are on one side and she is on the other. You will want to fight for him, for yourself, for your relationship. This is a trap, because nearly every problem you have with a difficult ex is largely due to him not knowing how to handle her.

Here's an example:

𝕁𝕦 When Janet moved in with her divorced boyfriend Leo, Leo's ex would hang up the phone when Janet answered it. The ex was still upset that Leo had divorced her and started seeing

Janet. Other times, she would rudely demand to talk to Leo, and even badmouth Janet to Leo. The ex's behavior annoyed Janet, who began feeling resentful. Leo told her not to take it personally, that his ex has always been "a bitch."

In this example, Leo's ex (an Angry/Difficult Ex) is behaving inappropriately. But so is Leo: he allows his ex to treat his partner disrespectfully, and he reinforces his ex's behavior by taking her calls. Leo should ask his ex to stop the rude behavior and comments, and then refuse to speak to her if she doesn't comply. If they have children and must communicate, he can do so by e-mail.

Here's a different example:

🔖 Kari's divorced boyfriend Mitch was frustrated with his ex. Mitch would make plans to pick up his kids and spend time with them, and then his ex would get angry at Mitch and refuse to release the kids at the last minute. Mitch walked on eggshells with his ex in order to avoid angering her, feeling that he had to do that if he wanted to see his kids. It angered Kari that Mitch's ex manipulated him and used the children as pawns to punish him. At times, Kari would get angrier than Mitch would.

Mitch's ex (also an Angry/Difficult Ex) is behaving inappropriately: she puts their kids in the middle of their conflicts and doesn't recognize that the children need time with their father (two divorce no-nos). However, Mitch is ultimately responsible for getting this situation under control. He needs to go to court and ask for fixed parenting time with his children and stop relying on his ex's moods. Flexible parenting-time schedules work for reasonable people only. Mitch owes it to himself and his kids to get this situation taken care of a soon as possible.

Here's another example:

🐾 Janna moved in with divorced man Nate after dating him for a year. Nate and his ex had two children together, and the ex seemed like a nice person. However, once Janna moved in, she began to see how dependent Nate's ex was on Nate. She called all the time about small things, such as what size shirts to buy their son and how much TV the kids should watch. She constantly sought Nate's help with everyday things like doing her taxes and fixing her car, and would drag out discussions about such matters as their daughter's college plans (she was twelve). Janna found her patience wearing thin and complained to Nate. Nate told Janna to stop being jealous.

Nate's ex, an Ever-Present Ex, had not learned to take care of herself after their divorce, and still looked to Nate to help her with things she should handle for herself. Nate only reinforced this behavior by rescuing her. Nate and his ex were continuing roles they'd played in their marriage. Although Nate's helpfulness is kind, it isn't appropriate once he's involved with a new woman. Janna's frustration was justified—who wants to be with a man who's constantly taking care of another woman? Nate needs to "cut the cord" and encourage his ex to figure things out for herself.

It's always a wake-up call to realize that your man has an Angry/Difficult or Ever-Present Ex, but it's an even bigger wake-up call to realize that he has no idea how to deal with her. Here are some typical signs that he mishandles her:

- He ignores her rude, bitchy, or manipulative behavior.
- He ignores it when she is rude to you.
- He gives in to her demands to "shut her up" or "keep her happy."
- He avoids dealing with her at all, letting problems get bigger.
- He gets angry with her and argues with her.

- He rescues her by helping her do things she could do herself or pay someone else to do.

The worse he is at dealing with her, the worse things will be for you and for your relationship. You want a man who knows how to handle his ex. However, a man who is willing to learn (quickly) is worth giving a chance as well. Overall, don't blame his ex for things he has control over. Your relationship is with him, not her, and he's the one you need to focus on when it comes time to solve problems.

Problem 5: You Have Big Shoes to Fill

When your partner has an Ever-Present or an Angry/Difficult Ex-wife, you may ask yourself, "What was he *thinking* when he married her?" In these cases, you can probably see how you may be a better partner for him than she was. However, some of you may find yourself wondering if you "measure up" to a divorced man's ex-wife. Although this can happen any time you date a man who's been in relationships before he met you, it can be more powerful when he's been married, for a couple of reasons: (1) he married her, which suggests he had strong feelings for her at one time, and (2) unlike an ex-girlfriend, an ex-wife may still be linked to him via children, or simply because he pays her money each month. When you step into the life of a divorced man, the following are some reasons you may feel that you have big shoes to fill.

She broke his heart. Although the end of any marital relationship is painful, men don't easily forget when a woman they love leaves them. The relationship ended before he wanted it to, and before he had a chance to see what wasn't right about it. Thus, there's a risk that you won't measure up to what he lost. The good news: a worthwhile man will grieve his loss and figure out why the relationship didn't last, regardless of who left whom. Avoid getting involved with him until he's finished this process.

She was unusually attractive or successful. Perhaps she has a powerful career, noteworthy accomplishments, or is simply beautiful—you may wonder if you measure up in his eyes. The good news: you must be pretty noteworthy yourself, or he wouldn't choose to be with you after having been with someone successful or attractive. More importantly, *you* must feel you measure up, because it's your opinion of yourself that matters most.

She was well-liked. If his friends and family really liked her, it will be more difficult for them to let go of her and embrace you. The good news: if they have the ability to like her that much, they will do the same for you, over time.

She had his children. Kids can give her a certain clout with him and his family, because all families value kids and she is their mother. Like many women, you may feel left out or undervalued because you don't share offspring with your divorced man, especially if you marry him. The good news: men want a good woman, not a baby factory. Besides, if things work out, you two can have your own children!

On the other hand, there are some situations that make you feel even more welcome in his life. If his ex had some less-than-ideal qualities, you may be especially appreciated by him as well as his extended family.

ᔑᕽ Cheri met divorced man Tim on an Internet dating site. Tim and his ex had no children, so he didn't talk much about his ex. However, one day Tim took Cheri out to eat at a local restaurant, where they happened to run into his ex. Cheri was surprised when Tim's ex gave her a once-over and then ignored her entirely, commenting to Tim that he'd "finally found someone." Tim told Cheri later that she treated everybody that way, including his family. Once things got serious with Tim and she met his parents and extended family, they welcomed her warmly because they liked her so much better than his ex.

However, regardless of what his ex is like, it's important to remember that he chose you for a reason—you have what he wants now. Two things cure the "big shoes" feeling: the first is knowing that you're better for him than she was. Note that I said "better for him," not "better than she was." There is no competition; relationships are about finding the right partner for you. The second is time. If you experience feelings of inadequacy that don't subside, you need to explore why. You shouldn't have to feel like you're in someone else's shadow.

NINE

The Five Rules for Dealing with His Ex

As discussed in Chapter 8, sometimes you can encounter problems with the ex when you date a separated or divorced man. Now that you're acquainted with these problems, here are a few guidelines for tackling them.

1. Be polite.
2. Minimize her involvement.
3. Establish boundaries.
4. Protect yourself.
5. Be curious, not obsessive.

Rule 1: Be Polite

Unless his ex is totally out of his life, you will eventually have to interact with her. Although your partner should be the one communicating with his ex, there may be times when you have to deal with her. No matter what type of ex he has, you want to treat your interactions with her like business transactions—be polite, but reserved. This establishes a rapport with her that is based on strength and respect. You set the example—even though she knew him first, you're with him now, which puts you in a position of power. Even if she seems a little cold at first, keep trying. Once she sees that you are comfortable with her, she should relax and feel comfortable with you. However, depending on what type of ex she is, you may need to tweak your manners when dealing with her.

In special cases, you may be able to have a more friendly relationship with a Polite or Absent ex. If she is inclined toward a friendlier relationship, feel free to encourage it. But it isn't a good idea to become close, as the main thing you have in common with her is him, and talking about personal things with her may cause problems down the road. Enjoy it, but keep your boundaries clear.

With the Ever-Present ex, you still want to be polite, but it's more important to keep a little distance. A business-like attitude shows strength while still encouraging goodwill. She is less likely to manipulate you and your partner or intrude on your time if you make your boundaries clear from the start.

When interacting with an Angry/Difficult ex, a businesslike approach is essential. This is a more powerful tactic than trying to be nice and win her over, which only encourages her disrespect, or going to the other extreme and being cold or unfriendly, which only confirms any preconceived notions she has about you and gives her an excuse to be rude. The best solution is to stay neutral.

However, if you find that polite and businesslike just isn't working, and his ex displays rude behavior, you will have to play hardball. Although it is *his* job, *not* yours, to deal with his ex, you can't avoid answering your phone or your door because you dread contact with someone who doesn't like you. Many experts tell women whose partner has an Angry/ Difficult ex to "see things from her point of view," to "kill her with kindness," or to ignore her rude treatment. This is bad advice—tolerating rude behavior sets a precedent for how she treats you in the future. However, arguing or fighting with her is no better, because that's what she wants. The solution? Cut her off.

Here are some examples:

- If she's rude on the phone, tell her in your most business-like manner to call back when she can speak respectfully, and hang up. Repeat until she gets it right.
- If she's rude in person, walk away, and avoid being around her in person.
- If she's rude at your front door, close the door.

Remember: she doesn't have to be friendly, just neutral. She doesn't have to like you—but she needs to keep her behavior in check. If she calls and coldly asks for your partner, don't worry about it. The important thing is that she's not rude.

These rules still apply even if they have children. If you live with him and she values speaking to her children while they're at your house, she'll clean up her act. However, your partner must step in and lay down ground rules for her if she calls or comes to pick them up. If she senses at all that he will put up with her rudeness, she will have a lot more power, and you will be all alone, fighting with someone you wouldn't even know if it weren't for him. His stepping in is even more important so that an Angry ex doesn't try to claim that you are trying to prevent her from seeing her kids. Your goal is to be treated decently, not to deny access to her kids—thus, both you and he should communicate that to her.

An important piece of advice to remember is that if your partner and his ex have kids, show her through your actions that you know she's their mother. When she calls, say, "Johnny, your mom's on the phone." When she's around, don't hold on to the children because they're on your partner's parenting time. Step back. And never tell her how to handle the kids. Imagine if you had kids and your ex had a new woman who acted as if she owned them. You would likely feel threatened, and people often act rudely when they feel threatened.

Rule 2: Minimize Her Involvement

What makes a Polite or Absent ex so easy to deal with? She isn't around that much. Ever-Present or Angry/Difficult exes are around *too* much. The good news is that your partner has control over that. You should not have to avoid all contact with his ex, and you should not ask him to do so. However, an uninvolved ex means less conflict for everyone, and his priorities need to be you and his children, if he has them, and making you and the kids feel comfortable.

There are several ways an ex may have more involvement in his life than you would prefer:

He is still separated or getting divorced. In these cases, he and his ex are still legally connected, which increases her level of involvement. At this time, there's little you can do about that, but he can still minimize her involvement and shield you from any unnecessary interaction with her.

He has children. Children increase her involvement, and make it permanent. However, while she will always be their mother, this certainly does not mean that you must tolerate an Ever-Present or Angry/Difficult ex intruding upon your lives in inappropriate ways. He must learn to handle her.

He and his ex haven't "cut the cord." Perhaps they still talk on the phone often, or she lets herself into his house to get the kids, or he plays Mr. Fix-it at her house.

Conflict. Conflict, regardless of who instigates it, means greater involvement.

During the dating phase, pay attention to his involvement with his ex. If you find that he hasn't trimmed down her presence in his life to normal necessities, wait and see if it changes once you two are established as a couple. If it doesn't, and you and he become more serious, explain to him that you're glad he has a working relationship with his ex, but that you feel like you are having a relationship with a man who has another woman in his life. Encourage him to keep up the good relations, but to minimize her involvement in your lives.

He can accomplish this by doing the following:

- He should encourage her to phone only for child-related issues (if there are children) or for the occasional social call. He can do this by not taking her calls, and calling back only if necessary. If she doesn't take the hint, he should be more explicit.
- He should ask her to use e-mail more often.
- If you and he live together and you don't have an ideal relationship with her, he should have her call his cell phone when a phone call is necessary.

- He should ignore her calls while he's spending time alone with you. If she has to discuss something important, she will leave a message.
- He should suggest that, when possible, they exchange their kids at school to minimize going to each other's houses. In other words, Mom drops off the kids at school in the morning and Dad picks them up at the end of the day. Many courts recommend this method—it prevents problems.
- He should encourage her to find someone else to help her with her home, car, or personal problems.

If he values your relationship, he won't mind making these changes. If she is too involved, you will begin to feel invaded, and resentful. This will only get worse if your relationship gets more serious, so try to work with him to nip it in the bud.

What if He's Still Separated or Getting Divorced?

These men can still minimize their exes' involvement to the necessities, such as dividing up their belongings, dealing with divorce issues, handling the children, etc. This is the business of ending a marriage, and may require more phone calls, e-mails, or meetings.

However, some men feel they must accommodate their exes beyond this level, and wind up doing favors for them or otherwise behaving as if they are still together. Again, doing favors is fine for the single guy, but a pattern of such behavior is inappropriate when he has a new girlfriend. In this case, he basically has two women in life, even if he's only having sex with one of them. Unfortunately, when the new woman complains, he may respond by saying, "She is still my wife."

Your answer to this should always be, "If she's still your wife, then I can't be your girlfriend!"

Rule 3: Establish Boundaries

Ah, boundaries. We've all heard of them, but what exactly are they? Boundaries are limits; they protect us and help guide our behavior in our relationships with others. Think about the boundary between two countries—the moment you cross over that line, you are in foreign territory and bound by the laws of that country. Boundaries in personal relationships are murkier, and sometimes you don't know where those boundaries are until you've had them crossed. Personal boundaries keep you from feeling invaded, run over, or swallowed up by someone. They help you maintain not only your space (physical and emotional), but also your rights (physical and emotional). A person with poor boundaries often lets others take advantage of him or her.

In Chapter 3 (on separated men) and Chapter 4 (on divorcing men), I emphasized that the boundaries of these relationships are unclear, and that unclear boundaries equal trouble. During separation or while divorcing, a man is free to date you but is still "married" (i.e., legally bound to another woman). Thus, both women have certain "rights" with him, creating a boundary minefield. With divorced men, the boundaries are clearer. However, some men don't have the best relationship boundaries, and may let the ex spill over into his "territory." When they have children, boundaries become a stickier issue because he must maintain a co-parenting relationship with his ex. Thus, it's important to establish good boundaries— and here are some guidelines for doing so:

Your relationship with him is yours. Any time your relationship progresses beyond casual dating and into exclusivity, you should take priority over his ex. She should only be a peripheral part of his life. This doesn't mean he can't be friends with her—it means that he should make it clear, to you and to her, that you are his priority. He shouldn't be on the phone with her all the time, interrupting time with you to answer her calls, spending his spare time fixing her car or toilet, or giving her money beyond agreed-upon child support or maintenance. These rules apply even when they have children together.

Your home is yours. Even if his home used to be hers, once he's in a relationship with you, she should not have a key to the house or walk in as if she's family. This is especially true if you're living there, but also applies when you begin staying over. And yes, the rule applies even if he has kids and they are at his house. There are many accounts of ex-wives waltzing into a man's house while his girlfriend lives there—this is wildly inappropriate. He should also establish rules for when she calls (for example, not too late at night or early in the morning) and how often she calls (for example, only for important issues).

The kids are hers. When it comes to the kids, let him and his ex handle them. No matter how close you become with him and the kids, they are still her kids. In live-in and marriage situations, women often take over responsibility for a man's children and deal with his ex-wife regarding the kids. This is not appropriate—let him do his job. It will take pressure off you, and show her that you know the kids belong to her. It also shows the children that you aren't trying to take their mother's place.

The ex is his. You should not have to deal with his ex for anything other than occasionally greeting her on the

phone. One woman I spoke to has a partner who hates his
ex, and he always avoids her when she calls. Predictably,
the ex gets annoyed and starts bothering this woman, trying to get information about the kids. Stay out of the
middle—let him handle it.

Rule 4: Protect Yourself

Unfortunately, some ex-wives are unhealthy people, and
these women may do some very undignified things. This
type of woman ultimately only hurts herself and shows
everyone how desperate she really is. However, occasionally
an Angry/Difficult ex can cross the line and do things that
are threatening to you, or even illegal. In these situations,
good boundaries and proper perspective aren't enough—you
must take measures to protect yourself.

Here are examples of when you need to protect yourself
against the actions of an ex:

- She harasses you by e-mailing you or phoning you, at
  home or work, with name-calling, threats, or other similar behavior.
- She harasses you in person.
- She threatens to hurt you in any way.
- She steals from you, assaults or attempts to assault you, or
  defaces your property.

For many people, the typical response to this type of
behavior is to ignore it. Separated and divorced men can be
especially immune to this behavior, for a couple of reasons:
they tolerated her mistreatment for years and are just glad to
get away from her, and they probably never learned how to

handle her insanity. So these men do nothing, hoping she will go away, and then ask you to do the same.

This response is *totally wrong*, for two reasons:

1. Your lack of action will only encourage her to continue harassing you.
2. Her behavior may escalate, putting you in danger.

Thus, two things must happen. First, he must deal with her behavior, and not let her get away with harassing you in any way. Second, you must protect yourself.

Here's how:

- Keep a log, with dates, of everything she does that is abnormal in any way, even if it's just rude behavior.
- Keep copies of any offensive e-mails, phone messages, or other evidence of bad behavior.
- If she does anything patently illegal (steals from you, assaults you, threatens you), go to the police and file a report. Try not to be emotional or hysterical—simply tell them what you've observed, and tell them that you feel you are in potential danger. Even if there isn't enough evidence to charge her or to warrant a restraining order, you've begun a paper trail, which provides a basis for charging her if she continues her behavior. Also, a visit from the police may be enough to show her that she'd better cool it. Here are a couple of real examples:

🕭 Sandra was involved with Mike, a divorced man with children. His ex was unhappy that Mike was seeing someone. One night, his ex broke into Mike's house, found Sandra's clothing and toiletries there, and proceeded to destroy all of Sandra's things. When Sandra and Mike discovered the mess, Sandra was horrified. Despite her horror, they decided not to call the police, for the children's sake. The ex continued to be a nightmare. Eventually, Sandra came to resent that Mike did little to check his ex's behavior, and broke up with him.

Mike, like many men, "handled" his ex by avoiding her and trying to ignore her crazy behavior, hoping she'd eventually calm down. Here was a perfect opportunity to check the ex's behavior, and nobody took it. When you date a divorced man with children, you must consider how your actions impact the children. But in this case, how did it benefit the children to allow their mother to get away with victimizing two important people in their lives? The children didn't have to be told what happened. Besides, a brush with the law might be the wake-up call she needs, controlling her behavior and thus making her a better parent. In addition, Sandra resented that her boyfriend hadn't done anything to protect her, and that she didn't protect herself when she had a clear chance to do so.

꙳ When Catherine dated divorcing man Alex, Alex's ex showed all the signs that she wasn't over him. Thus, Catherine kept a low profile. One day, Alex picked up Catherine and they went to the gym, then to his house. Alex's ex stopped by to drop off some divorce papers and saw Catherine. After she left, Catherine heard a door slam, and saw Alex's ex leave his car, get into her own, and drive away. Catherine, who'd left her things in Alex's car, checked them and found that her cell phone and underclothes were missing. She immediately called the police. Alex told his children that everything was fine, that he was just having a conflict with mommy. Alex's ex was convicted of theft, and was ordered to avoid all contact with Catherine. She never bothered Catherine again.

In this situation, Alex and Catherine held his ex accountable for her behavior. She therefore backed off, having learned that her behavior had consequences. Alex did not tell the children the gory details; the kids were not surprised by the conflict their father spoke of, as they'd seen their parents fight before.

Rule 5: Be Curious, Not Obsessive

Any time you date someone who's had a significant relationship, it's natural to be curious about his ex. You may wonder what kind of person she is and what she looks like, or you may even compare yourself to her. After all, you and she have one important thing in common: him. This type of curiosity can happen even if she's no longer in his life. Such curiosity is normal, and even healthy—knowing a little about his ex can tell you why things didn't work out with her, and therefore why they may work out with you. So feel free to indulge your curiosity: check her out, then let it go.

However, some women have a difficult time dealing with the presence of an ex-wife, or any ex. If you are one of these women, you are probably uncomfortable with the fact that the ex exists at all. Here are some signs:

- You refuse to meet her and you try to avoid all contact with her.
- You dislike that he stays in contact with her, even if it's only to deal with children or for the occasional phone chat.
- You obsess about her and compare yourself to her.
- You look for ways to denigrate her to your partner.
- You dislike that he has old photos of his ex, or other things from the time they spent together.

If you recognize any of these signs in yourself, it indicates that you are feeling threatened by his ex-wife. However, your feelings aren't about her at all, or about his relationship with her—they're about you: you don't feel secure enough about yourself and your role in his life.

This can be due to two factors:

Lack of boundaries. He hasn't established proper boundaries with his ex, and you're picking up on the fact that she has more influence with him than she ought. For example, he still talks with her often, fixes things at her house, or speaks fondly of her. In this case, your feelings of curiosity or insecurity will increase. You need to talk to him about his behavior, using the guidelines in this chapter. If he doesn't change, you will need to walk away, as you will never feel secure in the relationship.

You think you don't measure up. He is behaving properly, but you feel threatened by the ex because you feel you come up short when compared with her. In this case, try talking with a therapist about your fears, or they will interfere with your relationship.

Obsessing about the ex only hurts you and your relationship. Talking with a therapist will help, but in the meantime here are some things to remember:

- Being with her helped make him the man he is now—i.e., the man who wants to be with you. That's the beauty of divorce—it teaches us to pick a better one next time.
- Relationships are life experiences, not possessions. Relationships teach us how to love, deal with conflict, and learn what our needs are. He needed that experience with her in order to be with you.

- Think about what you have to offer—if you don't think you have what it takes to make him happy, then why bother with him?

No matter what type of ex-wife he has, she doesn't have to be a problem as long as he can manage her. If he doesn't know how, try suggesting some of the methods you learned in this chapter. However, if he won't change how he deals with a difficult ex, you won't be happy with him.

TEN

Parents Are Forever: The Kids

📣 Marianne met Donald at a church she had just begun attending. They hit it off immediately—they had similar beliefs, values, and backgrounds. The only obvious difference between them was that Donald was divorced with two sons, aged nine and thirteen. Marianne had never been married and had no children. But she felt Donald was perfect for her, as she did not want to have her own children and liked the idea of "marrying into" an established family. They married six months later.

The trouble began soon after. Although Donald's eldest son was quiet and kept to himself, his younger son, Cody, had some behavioral problems. Cody acted out in school and at home, disobeyed the rules, and rebelled against Marianne's authority. Donald, not understanding the root of Cody's behavior, alternated between punishing him and ignoring him. Marianne tried to fix the problems, but her efforts only seemed to make things worse. Soon she became resentful of Cody's behavior, which created marital problems between her and Donald—Donald felt Marianne worried too much, and resented her criticisms of Cody and of how he handled Cody. After a year of marriage, things had not improved, and Marianne moved out.

Although many women marry a man with children and have things turn out fine, this story illustrates how children can potentially impact a relationship with a divorced man.

The Importance of Children in a Relationship

We have covered in detail how not all separated and divorced men are created equally. One factor that differentiates one divorced man from another is children: a man with kids is in an entirely different category than a man without kids. In fact, children provide enough challenge to give relationships with divorced fathers a high Difficulty Index. Why is this? Because parenting is a lifetime obligation, and one of the biggest commitments a person can make. Not only must a parent raise, care for, and support a child for at least eighteen years, but parenting also forces people to change how they think, behave, and live. When you date a man with children, you too will be affected by the responsibilities that come with children. Moreover, if you move in with or marry him, your life will change considerably.

However, when dating, many people underestimate the realities that come with children. A man with children may get involved with a woman without fully realizing how her life is impacted by his children, or how his children's lives are impacted by her. Likewise, women who get involved with men with children may not understand the responsibilities that come with children, unless they have children of their own.

Moreover, marriage to a man with children has its own set of challenges. If you want a detailed account of all that it entails, read *The Courage to Be a Stepmom: Finding Your Place Without Losing Yourself,* by Sue Patton Thoele, and *Stepparenting,* by Jeannette Lofas.

Here is just one statistic regarding women who have married men who have children: According to the Stepfamily Foundation Web site (*http://www.stepfamily.org*), a Boston University psychologist researcher reported that of the career women who had married men with children, more than 75 percent of these women said that if they had it to do over, they would *not* marry a man with children.

Sobering words. However, any warnings regarding dating men with children found in this book are *not* due to any belief that children are bad, or difficult. The challenges that come with dating a man with children are rarely about the children themselves—instead, the challenges stem from the realities that come with the children, and how the adults in their lives deal with these realities. The problems presented in this chapter are based on the experiences of countless women. Overall, children are the *most important* factor influencing your relationship with a separated or divorced man—therefore, a relationship with a man with children deserves serious consideration.

All of that said, there is no reason to run and hide if you meet a man who has children. Before you toss this book down and go throw away that cute divorced father's phone number, remember this: just as all divorced men aren't created equally, the same goes for men with children—there are many factors that determine how challenging a man with children will be. This chapter will present the problems that accompany men with children, and offer guidelines on how to date these men.

Custody Versus Parenting Time

There are two concepts that are fundamental to all divorced men with children: custody and parenting time. People often use these two terms interchangeably, but they are not the same thing.

Custody

Custody refers to who has the legal right to decide how a child is raised. For example, the custodial parent can decide where a child goes to school, what doctor he or she goes to, or what religious beliefs he or she is raised with. Thus, one parent has sole custody, or both have joint custody. *Split custody* refers to splitting up the siblings: mom has custody of one child or some of the children, and dad has custody of the other or others.

Parenting Time

Parenting time refers to what percentage of time each parent gets with the child after the divorce: for example, 50-50, 70-30, and so on. Thus, one parent may have sole custody, but the noncustodial parent still sees the child on a regular basis. Both parents may have joint legal custody, but one parent may have more parenting time than the other. All of these details are decided, one way or the other, during the divorce. The traditional setup is that the mother has sole custody of the children, and the father has a certain percentage of parenting time with the children (often called *visitation*). Even today, the traditional setup is the most common one, where kids visit their fathers every other weekend and every Wednesday night.

However, the traditional setup isn't the hard-and-fast rule it used to be. Courts, custody evaluators, and the like are beginning to acknowledge fathers' rights and how important fathers are to children. Research has recognized that even though the role fathers play in kids' lives may differ from that of mothers, it is just as important. Thus, although today some divorcing couples may agree to the traditional setup, especially if the children are very young, a father who demands more is much more likely to get it. You will see more divorced men with joint custody and with parenting time closer to 40 or 50 percent.

Now that you know the basics, these next sections will cover the problems you may face while dating a man with children:

1. They don't like you.
2. You don't like them.
3. The children come first.
4. They will never be yours.
5. His fathering needs work.

Then, in the next chapter, we'll go over the rules for dating a man with children.

Problem 1: They Don't Like You

So you meet a man you really like, and the time comes for you to meet his children. He's told you how great they are and you are excited to meet them. However, when he introduces them to you, they aren't happy to meet you. After a few more tries, they seem uninterested in your presence—or worse, rude or disrespectful to you.

Following are several possible reasons for this type of behavior:

They're grieving the divorce. There is tremendous debate over how children are affected by divorce. Some say divorce affects children negatively no matter what; others claim children are happier when their parents are

128

happily married, and that an unhealthy marriage can do more damage to children than divorce can. However, good or bad, the children must grieve what they have lost and adapt to the changes in their lives. What sort of difficulties do children face when their parents divorce?

DIFFICULTIES CHILDREN FACE WHEN THEIR PARENTS DIVORCE

- They see their parents unhappy.
- They often have to change homes. For financial reasons, the family home may be sold. Even if it isn't, at least one parent must move, which means that the child has one new home to adapt to.
- Their emotional needs often get ignored because their parents are too wrapped up in their own problems. Thus, not only do they experience many changes in their lives; their primary source of support isn't there for them.
- In high-conflict divorces, the kids get caught in the middle of custody battles and power struggles over who is the better parent and who should have control over them. The kids wind up feeling like they have to take sides, care for a hurt parent, protect one parent from the other, or otherwise get involved in something they're too young to understand. This can have damaging effects.

Given these things, it isn't surprising that a child may not be thrilled to meet you initially. A child still undergoing this process will have a difficult time with a new woman, no matter who she is. It's best to take things slowly with children (see Rule 1 in the next chapter). You're most likely to encounter grieving children during the divorce and just afterward; if a few years have passed since the divorce and the kids aren't receptive to you, there may be other unresolved issues.

They're grieving their parent. In many divorces, one parent winds up getting the majority of the time with the kids, and it's not usually the father. The kids not only miss their father, but may fear losing him completely. This may sound silly, but children don't always understand things the way adults do, and sometimes their fears are warranted—some fathers move away or disappear after divorce. Conversely, in rarer cases, if Mom has given up custody and left the kids essentially motherless, you can understand why they're wary of a new woman.

They don't want to share. If they covet time with their father, they may not want to share him. This is especially true if they don't see him that often. This is more common in females, who may see you as the child's version of same-sex competition for his attention and love. One woman told me that her boyfriend's daughter would get jealous of her and try to demand her dad's attention when she was around. Another woman went as far as to say that she won't date a man with a daughter.

They're slow to warm up. Kids can be little shy, and this would prevent a child from feeling comfortable with you. In addition, many children may feel fear when seeing their parent with an unfamiliar person, and may not trust the person or understand the role that person will play. At eight years of age, I recall seeing the first man my mom dated after divorcing—I started crying and ran upstairs! Once I began to understand the situation and saw that he was a nice man, I warmed up to him.

They don't know how to talk to you. Kids can be impolite or may not know how to talk to an adult who isn't a parent or relative because they haven't been taught how. One woman briefly dated a divorced man whose teenaged son never acknowledged her, and then dated another divorced man whose teenaged son introduced himself to her and shook her hand. Manners must be taught.

Unless you are unkind or overbearing, their feelings toward you aren't usually about you. However, over time, if they don't warm up to you, you should consider whether or not it is worth it for you to stay in the relationship. Some women seem to take a love-conquers-all attitude, or a rebellious "I'm-not-going-to-let-some-brat-stop-me" attitude. Either way, they're missing the point—it isn't fun to spend time with someone who doesn't like you, and it doesn't provide a solid foundation for a future with this man.

Problem 2: You Don't Like Them

So what happens when you have the opposite problem—i.e., you meet your divorced man's children and find you don't like them? There are several possible reasons:

You're threatened by them. It is not uncommon for women to feel threatened by the amount of time and energy that children require. However, the duties he has to his children are inescapable. Additionally, when he has children he is never completely yours, as he is permanently bonded to children that he had with someone you don't even know. When you partner up with a man without children, on the other hand, you don't have to share him, and any children you have together are yours together. It's natural to feel a little threatened when you first contemplate a future partly shaped by someone else's children. Try to work through your feelings with a therapist. If you find you don't like to share, that's okay—just avoid men with children.

You think they're brats. Only biological parents and hopeful idealists like bratty children. Although every child can be bratty from time to time, consistent bratty behavior is never a good sign. This type of problem is a deal-breaker. Poorly behaved children will wear you down and wear down your relationship. If you make the mistake of marrying a man with bratty kids, they will chip away at your happiness and destroy your marriage. However, don't blame the kids: bratty behavior reflects deeper problems and poor parenting skills. Thus, a great guy with bratty kids may not be so great after all.

You don't like kids. In an advice column, a woman asked a dating expert for advice. This woman is dating a man with children, and she really likes him. The problem? She "can't stand children." Yes, this woman certainly has a big problem—she is trying to figure out the best way to tell this man that she really likes him but hates his children. It turns out there is *no* best way to say that. It may not be politically correct to announce it to everybody, but it's okay if you aren't a fan of children. Some women don't have a maternal instinct. Other women only like their own biological children. However, if you feel this way, don't get involved with a man who has kids. Find out up front if he has them, before you develop feelings for him. If you don't like kids and date a man who has them, everyone suffers: the kids suffer by being around someone who doesn't like them, Dad suffers because he cares for his children but you don't, and you suffer because you're stuck dealing with kids.

Problem 3: The Children Come First

When you ask the typical dating expert how to date a divorced man with kids, one of the first things they will tell you is "Remember that his kids come first." Most women, even those without children, can see the wisdom in this statement, so they nod and agree. However, everybody says this, but *nobody explains what it means*. Does it mean that he can't blow off his child's school play to go to Mexico with you? Or that you will always, in his heart, come in second to his children? These are very different questions. This discussion will be limited to *dating* men with children. Chapter 16 will discuss this issue as it pertains to cohabitation and marriage to a man with children.

The general rule is this: when you begin to date a man with children, his children will come first in his life. His commitment to his children is long-standing and permanent and they're dependent on him, whereas you are new in his life and your future with him is unclear. However, as your relationship becomes more serious, your status should increase. Once you begin planning a future together, you should rise to equal status as his children. In other words, you shouldn't take second place to his children when it comes to his heart and his time.

However, on a more practical level, there are some ways in which children will come first in a man's life. These "ways" have little to do with his love for you, and little to do with how serious you are as a couple—they're simply part of the realities of parenting.

The following are some examples of how children come first in his life, and how they shouldn't.

WAYS CHILDREN SHOULD COME FIRST

- His children are dependent on him, and thus he must meet their basic physical and emotional needs when they spend time with him.
- Children have school recitals, sports, and other activities where parental support is needed.
- Typically, he can't move away, because it creates instability for kids to change schools and the children need to be close to both parents.
- Children need care when they are sick.
- Children need some time alone with their father.

WAYS CHILDREN SHOULD NOT COME FIRST

- He should not break or interrupt plans he has with you for minor dramas (e.g., his child gets in an argument with Mom; his child calls him about something bothering him or her).
- He should never let them treat you disrespectfully.
- He should not attend only to their needs and ignore yours because you're an adult.
- He should not overindulge them or let them behave badly.

If you get involved with a man with children and he tells you, "Look, you need to know that my kids will always have to come first," beware. This often isn't about the children at all, but about his own guilt. A man who has good boundaries with his children knows that they have needs, and doesn't have to go around telling everybody how important his children are.

You will find that some parents suddenly become consumed by the children's needs during and after a divorce— they feel guilt over the divorce and work overtime to prove what great parents they are. Of course, these same people often fight with each other in front of the kids or badmouth the other parent. Moreover, if his kids' needs come first, why is he bringing another woman into their lives? The bottom line is that you should respect that his children need him, but know that your needs matter, too.

Problem 4: They Will Never Be Yours

Years ago, while having lunch out with my mom, I saw a four-year-old throw a tantrum and hit her mother in the face. Disgusted, I told my mom, "I don't want children!" She laughed and replied, "It's different when they're yours." This is a common sentiment—there's something about the bond one feels with one's own children that can't be duplicated. Otherwise, who would put up with the challenges of tantrums and hitting? This also works in the reverse: no matter how imperfect a biological parent may be, children often prefer that parent to a stepparent. Thus, when you get involved with a man with children, no matter how wonderful the children, your relationship with them won't feel like it would if the children belonged to you.

In addition to the limitations in bonding, his children won't belong to you in a more concrete sense. For example, a friend of mine who was engaged to a divorced man with a teenaged daughter disapproved of the skimpy clothes his daughter wore. "She won't dress like that when she lives in my house," my friend said. Unfortunately, my friend may not have a choice in the matter. Even if you marry a divorced man with kids, you will have a more limited role compared to what you'd have with your own children. For example, you don't get to decide where the children go to school, which doctor they go to, or how they are raised. This doesn't mean your opinion doesn't count—it means you don't make the final decisions. If you want to directly control how children are raised, you must have or adopt your own.

This topic certainly goes beyond *dating* a divorced man, but some women who get involved with men who have children have unrealistic expectations for how they will bond with his children, and how much influence they will have on his children. If you're just dating him, then you don't need to worry about this. But once you begin to consider a future with him, it is important to keep these issues in mind.

Problem 5: His Fathering Needs Work

Parenting isn't easy—most people fumble their way through it doing the best they know how. However, when you date a man with children, how he parents his children will have a tremendous impact on your relationship, especially if you're planning on a future with him. Divorced dads can be particularly inept as parents—even in this day and age, fathers are typically much less involved than mothers in the day-to-day realities of parenting. Thus, when divorce occurs, Dad is forced to become a more involved father, and he may not be prepared to cook, clean, or shuttle and discipline the kids. In addition, even a highly involved father may still feel overwhelmed by the demands of single parenting.

Overall, no father is perfect, and a newly divorced dad may take time getting into the groove of single parenting. However, if you date a divorced man with children and his fathering skills leave much to be desired, here are a few pointers:

- Don't tell him his fathering needs work. It will only make him feel inadequate.
- Don't give him advice—let him figure out the best way to handle his children. If he asks your opinion, give it briefly and neutrally.
- Never come to his rescue and help him parent—you gain nothing and he doesn't learn for himself.

However, although you can overlook an imperfect father, there are three types of divorced dads you should avoid:

Guilty dads. These fathers feel guilty for how the divorce impacted the kids, and will have a difficult time applying discipline or limits to his children. The guilty dad is afraid the children will suffer even more, or hate him, if he sets limits on their behavior. Unfortunately, his spineless behavior only makes things worse, because it doesn't provide the children with the rules and structure they need. Kids feel secure when their parents behave like parents and show that they're the boss.

Disneyland dads. These dads typically have their kids every other weekend or less, and they spend the entire time entertaining the kids with recreation, shopping, eating out, and the like. Although these dads seem fun at first, like guilty dads they want to win their kids' love instead of being parents. This always creates problems down the road. For example, it can force the kids' mother to become the "bad guy" who must apply discipline and deal with the more mundane aspects of parenting, such as homework and chores. This creates conflict between the parents, which puts pressure on the kids to take sides. Also, kids eventually lose respect for a Disneyland Dad, because they sense that he is trying too hard to earn their love.

Underinvolved dads. These dads don't spend much time with their kids, whether entertaining them or parenting them. These men are used to Mom doing it for them, or they just don't care for the rigors of parenting. When these men remarry, their new wives often wind up caring for the kids, which is bad for everyone.

However, before you find too many flaws in his parenting style, realize that men parent differently than women do, and provide different things to their children than women do. Fathers often put more focus on recreation and school performance, and less focus on things like neatness, nutrition, or safety. This is one reason kids need both parents in their lives. These gender differences in parenting style are being recognized by the courts, and have been incorporated into post-divorce parenting classes to facilitate positive co-parenting relationships. For you, the important thing is that your partner has rules for his kids, and is willing and able to enforce them. Kids need discipline and order as well as love, kindness, and fun.

ELEVEN

The Five Rules for Dating a Man with Children

If you are dating a man with children, you are now familiar with the challenges that come with that situation. This chapter will review some guidelines for navigating these relationships.

1. Take things slowly.
2. Adjust your expectations.
3. Accept only respect.
4. Assess his children.
5. Define your role.

Rule 1: Take Things Slowly

There are two ways in which you must take things slowly when you date a man with kids: (1) how long you wait to meet them, and (2) how you proceed once you've met them. Don't meet his kids until you are exclusive as a couple—that is, when you've moved out of the dating phase and into a relationship that shows promise. This minimizes the instability that arises from kids seeing many women come and go in their lives. However, don't wait until your relationship has become very serious—you cannot get serious with a man with children until you've spent time with his children. Once you meet them, take your time developing the acquaintance. Here are some tips on how to take things slowly.

Take your time getting to know them: You want to be friendly and show interest in them, but don't try to force a friendship with them. Let them come to you when they're ready.

Don't try too hard. Kids aren't dumb—they know when someone is trying to win them over. If you're too eager to please, they will pick up on this and it will make them uncomfortable. And don't try to buy their affections with gifts—kids can see through this, too.

Ask them about themselves. This works with most adults, and definitely works with children. They like people who are interested in them.

Don't hoard their dad. If your relationship goes forward, you'll have plenty of time with him. If you marry, you'll have your whole lives. Don't always be glued to his side when you're out with him and his kids, and make sure they have plenty of time alone with him.

🔊 Terri met Don through business dealings; she got involved with Don and they eventually got married. Don had a fourteen-year-old daughter, Gretchen—Terri liked her, and Gretchen liked Terri. Gretchen lived with her mother and only saw her father on occasion. However, every time Gretchen would visit her dad,

Terri was always at his side, so Gretchen never got to be alone with her father. Don wanted to make sure Terri felt included, and wasn't sophisticated enough to realize that his daughter needed some time alone with him. Terri, having no children of her own, didn't understand what Gretchen needed, either.

In addition to taking things slowly with the kids, don't forget to take things slowly with him, too. Children are probably the biggest challenge a divorced man can offer, so it behooves you to take your time getting to know him and how his children impact his life. And be circumspect about moving in together—once you live with him, your role with his children changes. Children who live with you are no longer just kids you hang out with; they become kids you are in charge of. This takes your relationship with his kids—and him—to a whole new level.

Rule 2: Adjust Your Expectations

If you've never dated a man with children, you may enter into a relationship with one without realizing that he is a different animal than the childless man. Unless he plays a small role in his children's lives, his children will have a tremendous effect on how he lives, which will likewise affect the time you spend with him. The impact of his children will depend on how much time he has them. A half- or full-time father will be quite busy, and your time with him will often include his kids. But even an every-other-weekend arrangement means that you won't be alone with him on his "Dad" weekends. Dads simply don't have as much freedom as childless men to do whatever they want. This is even truer when the children are young. Here are some examples of how his fatherhood will affect you:

- Unless he has older kids, they will need supervision, which means you won't be alone with him as much.
- He can't move away from the area he lives in, because the kids need to be with both parents. Thus, if you're involved with him, you can't move until the kids are grown.
- Kids occasionally get sick or have problems he must attend to, which may interfere with your plans with him.
- You will spend more time doing "kid" things, like watching Disney movies or going to amusement parks.
- When planning trips or vacations with him, he must work around his parenting schedule or make other arrangements for the kids.
- He must transport his kids to and from school every weekday they are in his care.
- When the children are in his care during the summer months, they aren't in school, and require more care.

If you don't adjust your expectations to the realities that children come with, you will find yourself disappointed. However, while some adjustment is okay, don't compromise what you need in order to keep him—it will only backfire later. If you prefer dinner out, late nights, and weekends away, then a man with children may not be for you.

Rule 3: Accept Only Respect

Unfortunately, some women are treated poorly by their partner's children. A man who lets his kids treat his partner disrespectfully is not only a poor father, he's a poor partner. Although no child is perfect, and occasional conflict is part of life, children should be taught how to behave respectfully toward you, and disciplined when they do not. This is his job, not yours.

When a child behaves poorly toward you, it's easy to blame the kid, but it is your partner's responsibility to teach his children how to treat you. And he should set the example: if kids sense anything less than respect from him, they will follow suit. When people tell you "Don't take it personally," that's good advice in principle, except that you *will* take it personally, and that doesn't solve anything. Over time, you will begin to build up resentment. Thus, learning not to take occasionally bratty behavior personally is a good skill, but a more useful solution is for him to get to the root of the behavior, and teach them to behave differently.

However, sometimes kids treat a parent's partner poorly because of jealousy—they see Dad's girlfriend getting all the love that they desperately need. One way to encourage respectful treatment from his children, then, is for him to build a good relationship with them. You can help by making sure they have lots of time alone with their father.

When Gina got involved with Matt, Matt's daughter Kylie clashed with Gina. When Gina and Matt moved in together, Kylie rebelled against Gina's authority. Gina would clamp down harder on Kylie and Matt would punish Kylie. Although Kylie got better about obeying, she never warmed up to Gina. This went on for several years, until Kylie moved in with her mother. The problem was that Matt didn't spend significant time with Kylie or express much affection toward her. When she acted out, he punished her. Thus, Kylie resented Gina for getting her dad's love and attention when she got so little. Gina only made this worse by trying to discipline a child who wasn't hers.

Set the example with your partner and his kids by always treating the kids with respect. If the kids do or say something rude, confront their behavior firmly but respectfully.

Show them that you won't tolerate their behavior, but don't resort to bad behavior yourself. Then follow up and talk with their dad about it, and make sure he follows through on dealing with it.

Rule 4: Assess His Children

When you get involved with a man with children, you cannot evaluate whether he is right for you until you evaluate his children. If you don't want them, then you don't want him. However, dating a man with children presents a quandary: meeting the children too soon isn't good for anyone, but waiting too long to meet his children is risky because you may become attached to him before you've had a chance to assess his children. Fortunately, you can find out quite a bit by simply asking him questions. You should consider the following questions when assessing his children, many of which you can find out before you ever meet them.

What is his custody arrangement? A man without legal custody has fewer responsibilities toward his children, because their mother makes most of the major decisions. In addition, it means he will have less parenting time with his kids.

What is his parenting-time arrangement? The more time a man spends with his children, the more they will affect his life (and therefore yours). An every-other-weekend dad is relatively independent, but a dad with 40 to 50 percent parenting time must be involved in the more mundane aspects of raising children, such as getting them to and from school, taking them to appointments and activities, and meeting their everyday needs. Although not typical, some men have 100 percent parenting time with of their children. Sometimes this can mean that Mom has died or has serious problems, which means the kids will likely grieve their missing mother. Whatever the situation, a man with full custody will have a lot on his plate.

How well-behaved are they? Poorly behaved children can be a deal-breaker. Often, poor behavior results from poor parenting. However, sometimes kids behave poorly after a divorce because they haven't worked through their grief. In other cases, some children have behavioral disorders, and will be a challenge no matter how skilled the parent. If you haven't met them yet and want to know something about their behavior, ask him what he finds challenging about parenting.

How old are they? Young children require much more care than older kids, which will have a greater impact on your time with him. If you date a man with a three-year-old and you and he marry, you will have to help take care of this child until he or she is at least eighteen. However, you have a greater chance of bonding with younger children because they'll grow up accustomed to your presence. If they're thirteen or older, you have less opportunity to bond with them, but they are more independent and only a few years away from legal independence. If his kids have reached adulthood, you won't have to take a parental role with them, and many of the child-related challenges are negated—for example, they aren't living under your roof, and the ex isn't as involved in your lives.

How many children does he have? The more children he has, the more complications there are. Not only are there more children to feed, clothe, and get to school, but each one has different needs. If the children are close in age and the same sex, however, they can play together. If he has more than one child, are they from the same mother? Half-siblings mean more exes to deal with, separate child support payments, and more complications.

Does he have boys or girls? You wouldn't think the sex of the children matters, but to some extent it does. Many people feel that boys are generally easier to raise than girls. In reality, both sexes have different issues. "Acting out" behaviors such as ADHD (Attention Deficit/Hyperactivity Disorder) and fighting are more common in boys, but anxiety and depression are more common in girls. These problems can range from mild to severe, although severe problems are much less common. Also, a number of women I interviewed reported that boys accepted them more easily than girls did, and felt that daughters compete with Dad's girlfriend or wife for his attention and love. A couple of other women reported that their partner's school-age sons wanted to impress them and would even compete for their attention. However, these are only guidelines—every child is different.

How do they treat you? Ideally, his kids will be friendly, respectful, and interested in you, and will get along with your kids, if you have any. On the other hand, they may ignore you (although don't be alarmed if they ignore you at first), or be impolite or rude. You may enjoy dating a man with children if his children like you, enjoy having you around, and treat you respectfully.

How solid is their relationship with him? Is his relationship with them distant or close? Is it smooth or rocky? Fun and light hearted or tense? A man who isn't close to his children will have more time for you, but you both may experience tension when the kids visit; this type of man probably won't make the best father if you want to have kids with him. If he has a rocky relationship with them, their time with him will be stressful, which will be difficult for you.

Once you've gotten all the information you need, both from talking to him and from meeting the kids, decide how comfortable you are with the situation. Unless you are relatively comfortable with all aspects of his having children—e.g., his parenting, their behavior—don't pursue the relationship beyond dating.

Rule 5: Define Your Role

When you date a divorced man with children, your role with them is simple—you're Dad's friend or girlfriend. But things get complicated when you get serious with him, and even more complicated when you move in with or marry him. For the purposes of this chapter, the discussion will be limited to the period of time while you are dating or having a relationship with him. Stepmothering roles will be discussed in Chapter 16.

When you date a man with children, your role is to be his partner, not his helper. Thus, while it's OK to help him out with the kids from time to time, you should not be doing the following:

- Babysitting them when he's working or out of town
- Driving them to school or to their activities
- Cooking, cleaning, or providing general care for them
- Advising him on how to raise or discipline them, even if he asks

Again, it's okay to help out from time to time, *if* you want to. But anything of this nature should be a favor from you to him, not something he expects or takes for granted. While you don't want to ignore the children or forget that children are a part of his life, and therefore yours, never take on his parental responsibilities with the kids—this is simply too much Input for too little Output.

Are You Cut Out for Dating a Man with Children?

Although many women are willing to date a man who has children, not every woman is cut out for it. In fact, several women have told me they could not marry a man with children or take care of someone else's kids. The important thing is that you figure out where *you* stand on this issue, and proceed accordingly. Realistically, you may not know where you stand until you get involved with one of these men and that's okay—just proceed slowly (and avoid moving in together or marrying) until you are sure it's right for you. Here are some signs that dating a man with children may not be for you:

You don't like children. Contrary to popular belief, not every woman loves children, especially someone else's children. If this is you, don't date a man with children and hope you will change with time.

You're "selfish." If you like your life the way it is and don't want to change it for the sake of children, then don't. The truth is, many people feel this way but won't admit it, then feel resentful of the children who enter their lives.

You don't have children of your own. Of course, this doesn't mean you can't date a man with kids. But if you do have children, it puts you on an even playing field with him because you understand the lifestyle children require.

And although the following items are more future-oriented, they're worth consideration:

You've always wanted a husband and children of your own. Living with and caring for children who aren't yours is a different ballgame. If you prefer a "traditional" family, stick to dating men without kids.

You like the idea of being "the lady of the house." Many women like to run the show (and the kids) in their home, but you have limited power when the children aren't yours.

You're hoping his kids will be a good substitute for having your own kids. If you're ambivalent about having your own kids, you should explore this issue in depth before getting involved with someone who has kids. You may find that stepchildren are just right for you, that you want your own kids, or that you don't want kids at all.

If you find that you aren't cut out for a man with kids, don't let anybody tell you that you're selfish or that you're throwing away a good man simply because he has children. The fact is, committing to a man with children is a huge undertaking—never take such a decision lightly. Saying "no thank you" is a million times better than saying "yes" and then feeling frustrated or miserable. Although, what if his kids are great? If you think you're cut out for a man with children, then lucky you! But if you aren't, great kids don't change a thing—move on.

You may be thinking, "But all the men my age have kids." If you find that's the case, you aren't hanging out at the right places. Not all men have kids; that's one of the benefits of being male—they don't have biological clocks and some wait until their forties and fifties to have children. In addition, you can date younger men, find men with grown kids, or keep looking. Don't settle for what isn't right for you. It isn't worth it.

One Last Point

This chapter may sound like one big warning about dating men with children. To some extent it is, but not because children are difficult or troublesome in and of themselves. The reason this book puts so much emphasis on the importance of children is this: children, more than anything else, significantly change the Input versus Output equation. In other words, children require large amounts of Input. Thus, the real question becomes: how much Output am I getting for my Input? If you get enough Output, then the relationship is probably right for you. If you aren't sure, don't do anything permanent until you are.

TWELVE

Friend or Foe?
Family and Friends

If you sat down and tried to imagine the problems you'd encounter when dating a separated or divorced man, you would probably imagine things like an angry ex-wife, kids who don't like you, or some other problem having to do with his ex or his children. His family and friends probably wouldn't even enter your mind. Yet, on occasion, his family and friends can provide their own set of problems. And when women encounter problems with his family or friends, they are often unprepared.

New and Old Alliances

Ex-wives and children play a central role in the separated or divorced man's life, and thus have more impact on his life. But family and friends matter, too—a supportive network of family and friends can go a long way in fostering your relationship. Likewise, a hostile group of family and friends can do a lot of damage. The bonds of family can be especially influential—we can choose our friends, but we don't choose our families, and thus we don't have the luxury of choosing a new family if they don't support us.

This section will detail just some of the ways that family and friends are important in a separated or divorced man's life, and how divorce impacts their behavior.

Marriage Creates Many Bonds

Anyone who's been married knows how true the old adage can be: When you marry someone, you marry an entire family. Marriage creates new family bonds, and they have names for these bonds: mother-in-law, father-in-law, sister-in-law, and so on. When the couple has children, these bonds are sealed, as the husband's family and the wife's family are related to those children legally and genetically. The children are "their blood." Bonds form with friends as well, because couples develop friendships with other couples and other families. If they have children, the children may grow up together. Thus, a separated or divorced man may have an extensive network of family and friends who have a vested interest in him, his ex, and his children, if he has them. If you date him, all these people will factor into his life, which means that they will factor into yours.

Divorce Impacts Everyone

When a divorce occurs, the legal bonds between some family members will change, but the emotional bonds don't change so quickly, and the blood bonds never change. Everybody feels the changes that come with divorce; a divorced man's parents will see their grandchildren less, their relationship with their daughter-in-law changes and may end permanently, his relationship with his ex's family changes, and all those family bonds that were formed must be redefined. A similar process happens with his friends; those who had friendships with both him and his ex as a couple must redefine those friendships. Friends may feel awkward until everyone finds their new place in the divorced couple's lives. Thus, everybody makes adjustments, and once they meet you, you will be a new "adjustment" for them as well.

Grief Is Important in Determining Their Behavior

As the other chapters of this book have emphasized, grief is a key concept in determining how a separated man and everybody related to him behaves during and after divorce. Family and friends are no exception, and their grief will determine how they deal with him and his separation or divorce, as well as how they handle you, the new woman in his life. If they are still grieving, they may have a difficult time with his seeing someone new. Everybody is different: some people make easy adjustments, and others have a harder time tolerating loss or change. Grief also depends on timing—the more recent the separation or divorce, the greater likelihood of grief.

Overall, family and friends are part of the separated or divorced man's life, and can impact your relationship with him. Some women may find that family and friends don't factor in at all when they date a divorced man. However, in this day and age many people don't live near their families; for this and other reasons, couples often don't meet each other's families until they've been together for a long time. Many relationships will have ended before the point where family begins to be important.

The more serious your relationship becomes, the more likely his family and friends will matter, for better or for worse. Family becomes most important when you marry him; then his family becomes your family. That's why it's important to evaluate family and friends, and how he handles them, *while you are still dating*, and not after you've gotten married and they're tearing your marriage apart.

This next section will cover some of the problems that can occur with the family and friends of a separated or divorced man.

1. They haven't let go of the past.
2. They disregard you.
3. They have divided loyalties.
4. He wimps out.

Problem 1: They Haven't Let Go of The Past

Sometimes when a man gets divorced, he adjusts to his new life before his family and friends do. Friends and family may not realize that a couple is experiencing problems until they announce they're separating. As a result, a divorced man has often moved on, but his friends and family are stuck in the past. This problem, like many in this chapter, applies more strongly to family than to friends. It seems strange that the people who were only peripherally affected by the divorce would be slower to accept it. However, it does happen, and there are several possible reasons for it:

1. Since his family and friends aren't the ones who got divorced, they have a harder time understanding the reasons for it, and thus are slower to accept it.
2. They've never been divorced, so they do not understand his reasons for getting divorced.
3. They have been divorced, and his divorce brings back unpleasant memories of their past experiences.

People cling to the past because the past is familiar—the changes that come with divorce are unfamiliar. Thus, if his family or friends haven't let go of the past yet, meeting them will be at least somewhat awkward because you are unfamiliar. The following are some signs that his family or friends have not let go of the past.

They display pictures of his ex. Many women dating divorced men get invited to his parents' home and find wedding pictures of him and his ex, or family pictures with her in them, displayed all over their home. This may feel strange, even annoying, depending on how serious you and he have become. The pictures make more sense if he is still separated or getting divorced. But the further he is from the divorce and the more serious you are as a couple, the more inappropriate the photos will seem.

They talk about his ex in your presence. Most people, when meeting their son's (or friend's) new girlfriend, know better than to talk much about the ex in front of her. It's just not polite. However, some people are surprisingly insensitive to this rule of thumb, and aren't aware of why they're doing it. This doesn't mean that his ex must be a taboo subject because you're around—it simply means that discussing her at length makes people uncomfortable, and puts the focus on her (and the past), rather than on you (and the present). Their commentary can take two forms:

- Positive comments. This occurs when his family or friends liked or remained friends with his ex and they talk about what she's doing, what was great about her, or otherwise reflect positively on her. Although it's good that they have nice things to say about her, and commenting on her once in a while is fine, consistent positive reference to her will make you feel overshadowed.

- Negative comments. This occurs when his family and friends weren't overly fond of his ex and reflect on her more annoying qualities. Negative commentary also includes overcompensating—i.e., when they try to find good things to say about her because they don't like her. For example, they state that she's moody and rude, but then add that she's a good mother to the children. Although less annoying than positive comments, negative commentary still focuses too much on her and the past, and not enough on the present.

If you are dating a separated or divorced man and his family or friends talk about his ex a lot, don't be too quick to label yourself as petty because you don't like it. Assuming you don't mind the occasional reference to her, your discomfort with their commentary is not about her, it's about wanting to feel welcome, rather than overshadowed by a woman he used to be with. The funny thing is, your partner probably has no desire to talk about her either.

They still refer to his ex as his wife. Old habits are hard to break. Family, friends, and even casual acquaintances of his may slip and refer to his ex as his wife. Even your friends may do the same thing. This not only happens when he's recently divorced, it can happen even after you and he get married.

🐾 When Julie met Erik, Erik was divorced with one daughter. After dating for two years, Julie and Erik got married. However, one of Erik's colleagues, who knew Erik had been previously married but had never met Erik's ex-wife, asked Julie, "What does Erik's wife do for a living?" Julie, recognizing what Erik's colleague meant, jokingly stated what *she* did for a living, rather than what Erik's ex-wife did for a living. Then, a few months later, one of her own friends did the same thing. Julie found this behavior bizarre.

Although Julie's example is a bit extreme, it isn't uncommon for people to use the word "wife" when it is no longer the correct word. This is more likely to happen when there are children, as people tend to associate "wife" with "mother." Overall, it's a good example of people's unconscious attachment to the past. The longer he was married, the greater the chance that this will happen.

Invitations that include his ex. His family, still hoping to retain some element of the family that no longer exists, may invite their son and grandkids over, and want to include his ex. They may do the same during the holidays. They will claim to do it for the children, but it's often about their desire to keep things as they were as much as possible. This behavior is more common during separation or divorce, when legal bonds aren't yet broken.

Overall, when you first become acquainted with his friends and family, some tendency toward such behaviors is okay. However, these behaviors should wane as you become more involved in his life, and you should expect greater consideration and standing with them as time goes by. If this doesn't happen, gently talk to him about it. A good man will take your side and want you to feel comfortable. He should discuss these issues with his family, and spare you the details if they aren't ready to move forward.

Problem 2: They Disregard You

Just as some people have a difficult time letting go of the past, other people have a difficult time embracing the future—in this case, the new woman in a man's life. Family and friends may disapprove of his divorce, wish for him to reconcile with his ex, or simply be unprepared for the presence of a new woman. If his parents aren't ready for you, they may try to carry on a relationship with their son as if you didn't exist. If your partner is still separated or getting divorced, this is more likely to happen.

If his family and friends are slow to warm up at first, that's okay. But when time has passed, you and he have become serious, and his family and friends aren't getting warmer, that isn't good.

Here are some signs that they are disregarding you:

You aren't invited to activities. If his family or friends invite him to their home or invite him to go out, and never invite you, they are disregarding you. You don't need to be invited to everything—sometimes they only want to see him. But it should not happen consistently after you and he become more "serious" in your relationship. Of course, this is assuming he wants you to join them—if he doesn't, then you have an altogether different problem!

They pay little attention to you. Perhaps his friends and family do invite you to events, but then they barely say hello, don't ask how you are, or don't make at least some effort to include you. It's possible they're just shy or socially unskilled; if that's the case, they should warm up with time. However, it may be that they aren't comfortable with you and are only doing the bare minimum to be polite so they can't be accused of being unwelcoming.

They're overtly rude. While the behaviors previously discussed aren't polite, they aren't overtly rude. Overtly rude behavior includes ignoring you when you speak, making rude comments, or other behavior that is clearly disrespectful.

🔊 Jeannette, a divorced woman with two daughters, was in a relationship with Bob, a divorced man with two sons. When Jeannette first met Bob's mother, who did not like that Bob had gotten divorced, his mother said nothing, and turned on her heel and walked away from Jeannette. It took Bob's mother a long time before she accepted Jeanette or her two daughters.

Jeanette and Bob's case is an example of extremely rude (and extremely childish) behavior, which, hopefully, you will never encounter. When his family or friends disregard you or behave rudely toward you, it's often out of misplaced blame—they blame you for his divorce, or for preventing him and his ex from getting back together. These people are not giving the man any credit. They are treating him as if he were a mindless automaton who would only leave his marriage for another woman. They are often emotionally immature, and looking for a scapegoat for their own pain rather than actually dealing with it.

They disregard your children. If you have children of your own, his family and friends should acknowledge them and try to make them feel comfortable. They should get the same treatment that you do.

Family and friends' behavior often depends on the nature of the divorce. If she left him, or wasn't someone they liked much, they will be nicer to you and more open to your presence in their lives. But if he left her, or they were fond of her, it will take longer for them to warm up. Ultimately, it is up to your partner to address this issue with his friends and family. He should not force you on them too soon, but he should not allow them to exclude you or disregard you in any way. If he doesn't stick up for you now, he never will, and getting involved with a man who won't stick up for you will cause you a lot of unnecessary pain. Problem 4 elaborates on this issue.

Problem 3: They Have Divided Loyalties

Because of the family and friendship bonds that formed when he got married, the breaking and redefining of those bonds with divorce may leave some family and friends with divided loyalties. When this happens, his family and friends feel loyalty toward him and toward his ex, which can be awkward when you come on the scene. Ideally, when a divorce occurs, family and friends support the person they're related to or friends with, and scale back their relationship with the ex-spouse over time. His parents and friends stick by him, her parents and friends stick by her, and although everyone tries to be polite, they know whose side they're on. However, this doesn't always happen. If they are close to both him and his ex, or they disagreed with the divorce, they may do one of two things: (1) they may try to stay neutral and be on everybody's side, or (2) if they are angry with him, they may switch to her camp.

The problem with family and friends who have divided loyalties is that you may not feel welcome around them.

❧ When Glen got divorced, his parents, who had supported Glen's troubled marriage for nine years, were sad that he chose to divorce. They were determined to avoid taking sides, and tried to provide equal support to Glen and his ex-wife. Unfortunately, the divorce was contentious, and neither Glen nor his ex was satisfied with this. Glen felt his parents should remain loyal to him, as he was their son, and his ex had treated him badly. Glen's ex, who opposed the divorce, felt she should get his parents' loyalty because Glen went against their wishes by divorcing her. Thus, Glen's parents were caught in the middle. When Glen began dating Brandy, they were torn between wanting Glen to be happy and wanting him to stay married for the sake of his family.

Glen's parents had divided loyalties, which made their relationship with Brandy difficult at first. Ultimately, it is up to your partner to shield you from this kind of mess, and not expose you to situations where you feel unwanted. He should talk with his family and friends and come to an agreement with them about what he needs from them regarding his relationship with you.

Problem 4: He Wimps Out

Countless women who are in relationships with divorced men have problems with his family, his ex's family, or his friends. However, even though these women are dealing with different kinds of problems, they have one thing in common: the man is nowhere to be found. Where is he, you ask? Hiding out, avoiding conflict, and letting his partner take the heat. Too often, if his family or friends behave inappropriately toward you, he may do little about it. This puts you at a huge disadvantage, because they are his friends and family—not yours. Unfortunately, his lack of assertiveness is not only annoying and unsupportive, but it also reinforces the problem.

Here are eight ways that a man "wimps out" with his family and friends:

1. He ignores problems instead of confronting them, hoping they'll go away.
2. He tells you to ignore them too, not realizing how much they bother you.
3. He tells you to not take their rude behavior personally.
4. He doesn't stick up for you or support you when conflicts occur.
5. He takes their side during conflict, and blames you for the problems.
6. He allows them to exclude or disregard you, and doesn't speak up on your behalf.
7. He's more concerned with their feelings than yours.
8. He seems to fear his family or friends, and avoids conflict by going along with them.

If he's doing any of these things, he needs to stop. The two of you should sit down and discuss the problems and decide what should be done, and then he should handle it. If they are rude, he needs to ask them to stop. If they ignore you, he needs to ask them to stop. If they talk excessively about his ex, he needs to ask them to *stop*. He should do this while you aren't present. He needs to be the buffer between you and them, and he needs to protect you from any hostility coming from them. Remember: you would not even know these people if it weren't for him. A man who wimps out when dealing with his family or friends will *never* be a good partner.

"But what if the conflict is partly my fault?" you ask. It's always good for you to look hard and figure out the role you played in any conflict with his family or friends, no matter how small. However, no matter who started it, he needs to stand by you, and he should lay down the rules for how they treat you.

THIRTEEN

The Four Rules for Dealing with Family and Friends

This chapter will cover the four rules for dealing with a divorced man's family and friends. Although these rules are designed for you to follow, they only work when your partner takes an active role as well.

1. Give it time.
2. Assess his family and friends.
3. Establish boundaries.
4. Accept only respect.

Rule 1: Give It Time

Just like his ex and children, your divorced man's family and friends require some time to adjust to the changes that come with his divorce. In most cases, there will be a period when his family and friends aren't ready to meet the new woman in his life. The length of this period will vary from person to person, but usually lasts longer for family than it will for friends. After this period, they may be ready, but may also be tentative or slow to warm up. This is especially true if he is still separated or getting divorced. Once the divorce is finalized, especially if the divorce took a year or more, his family and friends shouldn't be resistant any more. But if they are, there isn't much you can do except give it time.

It is up to your partner to determine the best time to introduce you to his family and friends. Friends usually have far fewer adjustments to make, and you will probably meet them much sooner. He should go ahead and prepare family and friends before introducing you, and he should ask if they would like to meet you. He should not be in a rush to introduce you—this is not because their feelings are more important than yours; it's to protect you from being exposed to people who aren't ready to meet you. The last thing you need is to feel unwanted, or like you're being "sized up" or scrutinized.

ℱ⤵ When divorcing man George met Dana, he fell in love with her and wanted to introduce her to his parents. George's parents were still adjusting to his divorce, and didn't mind meeting Dana, but they weren't ready to include her in more family-oriented events yet. George insisted on including Dana, as he wanted his parents to know how much Dana meant to him and he wanted them to see what he saw. George's parents relented, but they were reserved with Dana and talked about George's ex often. Dana, who had thought George's parents wanted her around, was offended and hurt.

George didn't follow Rule 1—he tried to force Dana on his parents. He was so happy that he couldn't understand why they wouldn't feel like he did. As a result, everybody felt uncomfortable. If George had simply taken his time and allowed his parents to get used to Dana in his life, he could have prevented these problems.

Take your time meeting his friends and especially his family, and give them time to get used to a new woman in his life. Once you meet them, they should be polite. Don't be in a rush to befriend them or to prove that you are everything his ex wasn't. Except for the most difficult of people, they will warm up to you over time. One last thing: giving them time doesn't mean tolerating poor treatment or disrespect—see Rule 4.

Rule 2: Assess His Family and Friends

As mentioned previously, problems with his family or friends may not reveal themselves until you and he have gotten more serious. However, despite this fact, it still behooves you to find out what these people are like, and how he handles them, as soon as possible. This will be relatively easy with friends, but may take more time with family, as he may not live near his family or see them very often. However, you can find out a lot of information ahead of time by simply asking questions. Asking questions won't get you as much information as actually spending time with the people themselves, but it can give you a good idea of what to expect. Here are some questions to ask him about his family and friends:

How do they feel about his divorce? The more they supported him getting divorced, the better off you are. If they were opposed to it, you should be more cautious with them, especially in the beginning.

Are they good friends with his ex? The closer their relations to his ex, the more divided their loyalties, and the more cautious you should be. They may have more difficulty making room for you, as she is still in their lives.

How did the ex treat them? If his ex behaved disrespectfully to any of them, that's bad for them but good for you. You don't have to worry about living up to a close friend. Instead, you can relax and focus on being yourself.

How did they treat his ex? Did she like them? The answers to these questions will tell you something about what type of people his family and friends are. If they didn't treat her well, that's a good sign they aren't the nicest people, even if she wasn't so great herself. Likewise, if she didn't like them, there's a decent chance they did something to earn her dislike. Another reason to be cautious with them.

Do they know he's dating you? How do they feel about it? If you've been dating him for a while and they don't even know about you yet, chances are he's hiding you from them for a reason (e.g., he fears they won't approve). If they do know about you, watch out for a negative, vague, or cautious answer to your inquiry. Anything less than general approval warrants your caution.

What's his mother like? Of all his family and friends, the one who has the most potential to affect your relationship is his mother. Because many sons are so concerned with pleasing a parent, especially a mother, her approval or disapproval of you could affect your relationship. When you ask this question, you may not get the whole story from him—but if he says something negative, then it's probably true. Beware, and keep your distance.

After you've asked the above questions, you will have some idea of what to expect when you finally meet these people in person. When you do finally meet them, assess the following things:

- How kind and friendly they are to you
- How kind and friendly they are to your children, if you have them
- How they treat him
- How much they talk about the ex, and what they say about her
- How consistent their behavior is with his description of them
- How their behavior changes over time

A bad set of family or friends can chip away at a relationship. In fact, it's a deal-breaker if he doesn't know how to handle them. However, bad family and friends aren't a dealbreaker as long as he knows how to handle them, stands by you, and doesn't allow them to mistreat you in any way.

Rule 3: Establish Boundaries

Oh yes, here's the old B word again: boundaries. Boundaries are just as important with family and friends as they are with exes and children. His family and friends may not be perfect and you or he may have occasional conflicts with them, but if you and he establish good boundaries, they will follow suit. Here are some major areas where he must establish boundaries with his family and friends:

- He should talk about you before he brings you out to meet them, and establish that you are important to him.
- If they show signs of hostility (e.g., disregarding you), he should speak with them in private and ask that they be polite and act appropriately with you. This shows them

where he stands, and will usually do the trick. If they resist, he will have to try stronger measures.

- If they persist in leaving up pictures of his ex or in talking about his ex, he should politely ask them to take down the pictures and avoid the ex topics. Again, asking for what he wants should do the trick.
- If his parents meddle in his relationship with his children or his ex, it is up to him to confront that behavior and deal with it.

Likewise, there are areas where you must establish boundaries for yourself regarding his family and friends:

- If you have a problem with how his family or friends behave toward you, you should speak to him, not to them. This doesn't mean you should tolerate disrespect (see Rule 4); it means that if you are uncomfortable with something they're doing (e.g., talking about his ex all the time), you should go to him. Then, he should talk with them about it, making it sound like a request from him, rather than from you.
- If his family or friends want to discuss his ex with you, humor them for a couple of minutes. If they persist, try to change the subject by making a segue into a related topic, or by asking them something about themselves. If you need to, just politely say that you feel awkward talking about someone you don't really know.
- If he has a conflict with his family or friends, or isn't close to them, they may come to you for advice, to vent, or for favors. Don't be tempted by their sudden interest in you; it puts you in the middle of his relationship with them. Ask them to talk with him, and ask him to deal with them in order to take the heat off you.

- While you should expect him to have boundaries with his family and friends, he cannot change who they are. If he asserts himself and asks them to behave respectfully but they choose not to, don't blame him for their behavior.
- If he is serious about you, he should support you. But don't expect him to completely disregard his family or friends if they're difficult people. If they're intolerable, let him see them on his own time.

Boundaries are important in relationships, but it takes time to form good ones. Don't worry if you make a few mistakes—sometimes we don't know where our boundaries are until *after* we've had them stepped on.

Rule 4: Accept Only Respect

One alarming trend I've noticed in my interviews and research is how much disrespect women will tolerate from the divorced man's family. This is more common during marriage than during dating, but it never hurts to be prepared ahead of time. There are two reasons women tolerate disrespect from people in his camp: (1) these women are often outnumbered and don't feel comfortable "taking on" his clan or (2) they want to preserve the peace, especially if there are children involved. However, in the long run, tolerating disrespect doesn't keep the peace, because it only engenders anger and resentment in you. Thus, if you come across family or friends who are rude or disrespectful, don't put up with it. How do you do this?

First, the most powerful thing you can do from the very beginning is try to get off to a good start by being polite and respectful. Set a good example for them, and be patient if they are slow to warm up. If you begin to see signs of problems such as those mentioned in Chapter 12, talk to your partner about it, and tell him how it makes you feel. Hopefully, he'll talk with them and nip the problem in the bud. If, after all this, you experience rude or disrespectful treatment from them, assert yourself and ask them not to speak to you that way. Stand your ground, no matter how they react. Your show of strength should do the trick. If it doesn't, more extreme measures are needed: walk away from disrespect. If you are at their home, tell your partner you need to leave. If it happens over the phone, inform them that you don't want to be spoken to that way, and hang up.

Don't make the two common mistakes women make:

1. Don't get into a brawl with them. Some people thrive on conflict, and fighting only feeds the fire and makes things worse. Besides, what is there to argue about? They were disrespectful, and you aren't putting up with it. Case closed.
2. Don't ignore their behavior and swallow your anger, and then complain to him how mean his family is. This only creates more problems. Assert yourself.

Fortunately, most of you won't have to deal with this situation. But for those of you who do, both you and your partner need to assert yourselves and accept only respect. Your man should stick up for you. If he can't manage to do that, then you will never be happy with him.

What if *Your* Friends and Family Are the Problem?

When you date a separated or divorced man, sometimes *your* family and friends are the difficult ones, not his. Perhaps they're overly concerned for you, or they disapprove of your dating a man with children, or they aren't very warm to him or his children. Just as he must deal with his family and friends and provide the buffer between them and you, you must do the same for him. Talk to them about him before you introduce him. If they express concerns, talk with them about their concerns—you may be able to put them at ease. If not, make it clear to them that he is your partner, and ask them to respect that. Also, don't lie to him about how they feel, but don't tell him details that would offend him, either. For example, if your parents aren't as warm about him as you would like them to be, tell him they're a little hesitant because they want to make sure their daughter is happy. Make sure he knows you're on his side.

Is He a Keeper?

Although you cannot fault a man for having less than ideal family or friends, you can fault him for how he handles them. A man who doesn't know how to handle his people, especially his family, will be a terrible partner down the road, so pay close attention to the signs:

Keep him	Lose him
If his family says something rude or embarrassing to you, he gives them a signal to stop and then speaks to them later about the issue.	If his family says something rude or embarrassing to you, he says nothing or acts like it's no big deal.
If there's conflict between you and them, he steps in and handles it.	If there's conflict between you and them, he steps back and lets you handle it.
If you complain about rude treatment from them, he takes your side and speaks with them.	If you complain about rude treatment from them, he blames you, tells you not to take it personally, or tells you to handle it yourself.

Keep him	Lose him
You feel like he's on your side.	You feel like he's on their side.
He stands up to them during conflict.	He backs down from conflict with them.
He cares for them but decides for himself what's best for him.	He's overly concerned about pleasing them or needs their approval.
Your relationship is serious and you're most important in his life.	Your relationship is serious but they're more important in his life.

Is there hope for a man who doesn't step in and take control of any conflicts that arise between his family or friends and you? Possibly. Often, many of us are taught to respect our parents, and for some, "respect" means putting up with poor behavior. Thus, men who don't step in during a conflict may do so only because they don't know any other way. The first time it happens, let him know exactly what he should do, and see if he goes and takes care of it. If his family or friends behave rudely again, see how he handles it. If he doesn't step in and stick up for you, you many want to reconsider your relationship.

FOURTEEN

Wolf in Sheep's Clothing: Money

Of all the challenges presented in this book, financial issues are probably the least worrisome in terms of dating separated and divorced men. However, money issues qualify as a "wolf in sheep's clothing" for a reason: they seem innocent or easily ignored at first, until one day, down the road, they bite you unexpectedly.

Money and the Separated or Divorced Man

Money is one of the top three things couples fight about (the other two are sex and children). Why is this? Money represents so many things to people: power, safety, choices, comfort, fun, status, reward. Having money, and more importantly, having control over money, gives people a sense of control over their lives. Of course, those who focus too much on money are missing the point—money isn't everything. However, to ignore financial details that will affect you, and thus your relationship, isn't wise.

So how does this apply to separated and divorced men? These men often have financial issues that never-married men don't have, and these issues can affect your relationship with him. Some of the financial difficulties that separated and divorced men come with include:

- Significant divorce costs (if separated or getting divorced)
- Debt left over from the marriage or the divorce
- Child support and maintenance payments (this is not including the regular costs that surround raising children)
- Credit problems from the marriage or divorce

Thus, separated and divorced men may be strapped for cash, even if they have well-paying jobs. When dating these men, you may want to go out and do fun things with him, or travel with him, and find that he can't do all those things you want to do. Over time, if you move in together or get married, financial issues will become much more important as you try to budget, plan your future, buy a house, and so on. Fortunately, although some financial issues can be problematic, most are not deal-breakers. However, one of your biggest enemies—i.e., the "wolf"—is ignorance. Many women aren't aware of the financial realities that separated and divorced men face, and can wind up surprised or resentful. Because money is such a touchy subject, women may avoid discussing money issues with men for two reasons:

1. Quality women don't choose a man based on the size of his wallet. Thus, many women ignore financial issues for fear of looking like gold-diggers.
2. Many women want to believe that love conquers all, and that finances can't get in the way of true love.

Money does matter and couples should always discuss finances when planning for the future. When dating separated or divorced men, a little education about the financial realities they face will go a long way toward preventing the old wolf from baring its teeth.

However, before examining money problems in greater detail, you must understand that his money issues will differ depending on whether or not his divorce is final.

Separated and divorcing men. Until the divorce is final, he is legally tied to his ex, and therefore so are his finances. He is financially constrained during this period; his money isn't entirely his, and the divorce and divorce-related issues will eat up a lot of his cash. In other words, he may not have the freedom to spend how he wants to.

Divorced men. Assuming they pay their bills, divorced men don't have to answer to anyone but themselves when it comes to money. But, as you will find in this chapter, they may have other financial issues and obligations to contend with.

The Four Money Problems with Divorced Men

1. His money goes to his ex.
2. Kids cost money.
3. He has debt or credit problems.
4. He's overindulgent.

Problem 1: His Money Goes to His Ex

One of the strangest things you may have to contend with while dating a separated or divorced man is watching a portion of his paycheck go straight to his ex-wife. This is especially inconceivable when they've been divorced for years. You may think, "Why is he paying her all that money? Their relationship is over!" Assuming he pays his ex alimony or child support (and not all men have to), you probably won't face this problem when you start dating him—in fact, at that point you probably know nothing about his finances. But once you move in together or marry, this issue *will* come up. After all, a chunk of the money he earns that would normally belong to the two of you may go to his ex-wife. Some people refer to this as "economic polygamy," a funny but somewhat disturbing descriptor. In other words, economically speaking, he has two wives to support: his ex-wife and his current wife. This can be a big pill for many women to swallow—they didn't do anything wrong, so why should they have to share resources that should belong only to them?

Because this is a potential hot-button issue, you need to find out all you can about what he pays to his ex-wife, and why. His payments typically break down into two different components: child support and maintenance.

Child Support

The purpose of child support is for divorced parents to share the expenses of raising children. Child support is calculated using a formula; although differing somewhat for each state, this formula is based on two factors: how much each parent has the children, and how much money each parent makes. The formula takes into account how much money is available from each parent (based on income), pools it together, and then redistributes it. Usually, the parent who has the greatest amount of parenting time receives child support from the other parent because he or she has to absorb more of the cost of providing housing, clothing, food, and child care for the kids. Typically, fathers pay mothers child support because mothers have the children for more of the time. Child support is usually paid until a child turns 18 or 19, but can continue through the college years.

What happens when mom and dad share 50-50 parenting time? Then, child support is based only on income. If the parents make the same amount, nobody pays child support. If one makes more than the other, the higher-paid parent pays the other parent—the greater the income differential, the greater the amount paid. Why? A certain portion of a parent's income is designated for the costs of children. For example: Mom doesn't make much, so her portion is $200 per month. Dad makes more, so his portion is $400 per month. Pooled together, their child costs are $600 per month. If they share the kids 50-50, this $600 should be split equally between households—thus, Dad pays Mom $100 per month to bring her $200 portion up to $300. The system is designed to prevent one parent from absorbing too much of the cost of childrearing.

Child support is often given a bad name. However, it's one of the few areas in divorce that is relatively fair and objective—the formula applies to everyone and no judge or lawyer can alter it. You may ask, "But what if his ex refuses to work in order to get more child support?" The courts will impute her with an income, based on her education, experience, and work history. Everybody is expected to care for their children, and the penalties for refusing to pay child support are typically severe. Finally, child support can change if parenting time or income changes, but it never goes away. Thus, if you marry a divorced man with kids, his child support obligations remain even if you and he have a bunch of kids together.

Maintenance

Also known as alimony, maintenance refers to one spouse providing the other with financial support that is unrelated to the children. This support can occur during separation, during divorce, and after the divorce is finalized. The purpose of maintenance is to provide the spouse, usually the wife, with support until she can provide for herself. Because women's roles have changed so much in the last few decades—that is, women are more educated, have more opportunities, are more inclined to have careers, and make more money now than they used to—maintenance is not awarded as often as it used to be.

Unlike child support, maintenance has no formula attached to it—there are only guidelines, which vary somewhat from state to state. Thus, the courts have considerable latitude in determining whether maintenance is warranted, and if so, how much and for how long. Contrary to popular belief, maintenance is not automatic. In fact, it is only awarded about 15 percent of the time. In addition, many men agree to pay maintenance—it isn't always ordered by the court.

There are several factors that go into determining whether and how much maintenance is necessary:

How long they were married. Long-term marriages (greater than ten years) tend to warrant an award of maintenance more often than shorter marriages.

She stayed home with the kids. This puts her at a financial and professional disadvantage; he had the greater advantage because he could concentrate on his career and get valuable job experience.

The financial resources of each spouse. She must demonstrate financial need in order to receive maintenance. Likewise, he must demonstrate the ability to pay, and cannot be ordered to pay so much that it would put an undue burden upon him.

The lifestyle she was accustomed to during the marriage. Contrary to popular belief, this is only one of many factors taken into consideration.

Her health and ability to work. A woman who has poor physical or mental health may need support for a long period of time.

Maintenance payments are usually temporary, and will continue for as long as he and she have agreed on, or as long as the court decides is needed to get her on her feet, through school, etc. Some states use the half-the-marriage guideline: i.e., if they were married for sixteen years, he pays her maintenance for eight years after the divorce. Also, maintenance usually ceases if the ex remarries or cohabits with someone, unless otherwise specified in the divorce agreement.

Many people find the concept of maintenance stupid. "They aren't married anymore! Why should he have to pay her anything?" The primary reason is that when two people get married, sometimes one person gains more financially from the marriage than the other. Here are some examples.

EXAMPLE 1

Dick and Jane get married and have children. Dick works and Jane stays home to care for the kids. If Jane has a career, she gives it up, at least for a while. If Jane never had a career, she has no time to get one now. Meanwhile, Dick is out working, gaining valuable experience and increasing his earning power. Jane's earning power stays the same or goes down because she's been out of the market for so long. If they divorce, Jane is relegated to a lower standard of living than Dick is. "Well, she chose to stay home." Yes, she did, but that's what they both wanted at the time. Someone has to care for children, especially when they are young, and sometimes it's cheaper to quit work and stay home than to pay for day care. Thus, Dick benefited from Jane's willingness to care for the children, and some maintenance may be appropriate to help her get back on her working feet.

EXAMPLE 2

Dick and Jane get married and have kids. Jane stays home with the kids while Dick goes to medical school. After he completes his training, they get divorced. Dick has an M.D. and therefore good earning potential; Jane has plenty of experience caring for kids, but nothing else to show for her sacrifice. Thus, he benefits more than she does, at least from a financial standpoint. Remember, with no one to care for his kids, Dick would never have gotten through medical school.

EXAMPLE 3

A variation of example 2 is that Dick and Jane marry and do not have children, but Jane works full-time to put Dick through medical school. If they get divorced, he winds up with a lucrative degree and a future, whereas she spent all her earnings to feed, clothe, house, and educate Dick. Dick would not have gotten through med school without Jane's support—at least not as successfully and not without accruing an enormous amount of debt. Again, Dick benefits at Jane's expense.

You've heard the saying "There's no such thing as a free lunch." These three examples illustrate that point: during the marriage, Jane's sacrifices resulted in Dick gaining more from the marriage than she did, at least on a financial level. Maintenance is a way of "leveling the playing field"—i.e., making the financial division truly equal. Thus, Dick got his "free lunch" during the marriage, and now he must pay for it. If people didn't get divorced, this wouldn't be an issue. Let's say Jane put Dick through med school and they stayed married. Eventually, Dick would earn good money, providing both of them a more comfortable lifestyle, and Jane would get something back for her investment.

However, there are times when maintenance is not necessary:

> ꜰ Karen married Quentin, who owned his own business and did well financially. Thus, Karen worked only part-time, and sometimes not at all, during the marriage. After six years, Karen and Quentin split, and Karen requested that Quentin pay her maintenance. She believed she was entitled to maintenance because Quentin made a lot of money and she felt she'd given him a lot during their marriage. However, in this case, maintenance was not awarded, because Karen was perfectly capable of supporting herself and did not sacrifice significantly for Quentin's gain.

Some women believe it's a man's job to take care of them forever, even after a divorce is over. The justification for maintenance is a complicated and controversial issue. If you are dating a divorced man who pays a lot in child support or maintenance, find out all you can about the circumstances. For your purposes, it's important to know the facts before you make any binding commitments to a divorced man. If he pays her a large sum and you disagree with the reasons, do not ignore those feelings and assume you're being shallow or greedy. As mentioned in the beginning of this chapter, money isn't always about money; it's about power and control. And you may find yourself feeling powerless if he agreed to pay more than he ought to. Think seriously before you commit to sharing his financial burden to his ex.

The good news? Most divorced men don't pay maintenance. And if he does, it's probably somewhat justified, and most likely temporary. If you date a man who must pay maintenance to his ex, it helps to think differently—instead of thinking that he makes $2,000 per month but must pay his ex $500, think of his income as $1,500 per month.

Problem 2: Kids Cost Money

Separated or divorced men with children have a financial obligation to those children at least until they turn eighteen and graduate high school. This applies even if he was never married to the mother of his children. The costs of children come in two forms: child support payments, which I described in Problem 1, and the everyday costs of having children around. This latter category includes:

- Daily needs such as meals and school lunches
- Periodic expenses such as clothing and school supplies
- Medical and dental care, in the form of family insurance coverage (which is *much* more expensive than covering just yourself), and occasional illness or accidents
- Child care for after school or during summer, or daily if the children aren't in school yet
- The costs of sports, hobbies, activities, and recreation
- Once the children reach age sixteen, a car, including gas and car insurance
- College, including tuition, books, and living expenses

Other child costs many people don't consider include larger mortgage or rent payments because he needs extra rooms for the children, greater vacation costs due to needing extra airplane seats and hotel rooms, and the cost of larger and safer cars to accommodate children.

Thus, if you date a divorced man with children, these are the standard expenses he will face. Unfortunately, the costs of children stay the same no matter how little he earns, so the man who doesn't earn much will be strapped for cash. This can put a damper on your plans, making it more difficult to go out and have fun, or to travel. However, while the financial realities that come with his children can be daunting, they are usually manageable.

Problem 3: He Has Debt or Credit Problems

Marriage, and the end of a marriage, can have some unpleasant financial fallout. If during the marriage he or his spouse spent excessively, lived beyond their means, or even experienced hard times such as a layoff, debts will accrue. By the time a divorce finalizes, he may have debts from divorce-related costs, including attorney's fees, custody evaluation fees, and other financial burdens he had to take on in order to divorce. In addition, very late or unpaid bills for either partner can wreak havoc on credit history for both spouses, making it difficult to buy a car, buy a home, or get a loan down the road. If a separated or divorced man has these problems, it may be his doing, but it also may be his ex-wife's doing. That's one of the problems with marriage—if your spouse is financially irresponsible, it will affect both of you.

Many debts and credit problems have effects that can last for years. Small credit card balances and attorney's fee balances aren't that big a deal, as they can be paid off. You may have to forgo eating at nice restaurants and other luxuries for a while, and these things shouldn't have much of an impact on your future with him. However, larger debts, unpaid bills, and credit problems are red flags, as they will impact your future together. Even if his problems are due to his ex, they will still affect your future, and his debts or bad credit may prevent you from buying a home together. You may have to be the "breadwinner" and put every purchase in your name, which puts a lot of burden on you for problems you did nothing to cause. Moreover, if he was part of the reason for the debts or credit problems, you put yourself and your future at risk by aligning yourself with someone who has these problems.

Some debt isn't worth worrying about, as long as it is paid off over time. Larger debts are worth your concern—if his debt results from furthering his education, and therefore his career, or something else that will "pay out," that's better than large debts that are due to overspending or other mishaps. The latter indicates financial irresponsibility, and you don't want to align yourself with a financially irresponsible person. Credit problems are a deal-breaker, unless he learned from his mistakes and proves that he is working to get his credit back up to where it needs to be.

Problem 4: He's Overindulgent

Divorce can leave some men with a guilt complex. They feel bad for divorcing, for putting their children or ex through difficulties, or for seeing their children much less than they used to. And sometimes they use money to "make up" for these losses.

This type of man may:

- Buy his children toys, clothes, or other things every time he sees them.
- Constantly take his children fun places to keep them entertained.

- Give his ex more money than he's required to.
- Give in to his kids' or ex's requests for unnecessary material things.

This man is in a tough position, because he, like most men, doesn't want to look cheap or uncaring toward the ex or kids. But a tendency to overindulge represents an attempt to absolve his own guilt, and does not actually benefit those he overindulges. Not only that, when he spoils his children with toys, clothes, and recreation, he becomes a babysitter with a big wallet, not a father. Fathering includes spending money on them and doing fun things, but it also includes teaching them, guiding them, and asking them to do the more mundane things in life, like helping with the dishes. Likewise, when he gives his ex additional money, he becomes her sugar daddy, which benefits nobody.

When you date a separated or divorced man and watch this happen, it can be very frustrating. You can see what he's doing, but you fear that complaining to him will make him angry. The only thing more stubborn than guilt is denial that his overindulgence is about guilt, not love or kindness.

If your man is overindulgent, and you value your relationship with him, you have to confront him about his behavior. Be gentle—tell him you understand that he cares about his children and wants to have fun with them, or that he wants to be kind to his ex, but that overspending on them will only engender disrespect in them in the long run. Tell him it makes you uncomfortable. If he cares about you, he will listen and make the changes.

If he's too stuck in his ways to change, you may have to walk away. Money isn't the primary issue here—overindulging his children or his ex-wife, whether with money or in other ways, is a sign of poor boundaries. Often, these men aren't effective parents because they're too busy trying to win the children's love. They probably won't have good boundaries with their ex-wife in other ways, either. As I've said throughout this book, poor boundaries equal trouble. Thus, don't ignore overindulgence if you feel it's a problem.

The Four Rules for Dealing with Money Issues

Now that you are aware of the main money problems that come with divorced men, here are some guidelines:

1. Assess his finances.
2. Don't rescue him.
3. Keep your job.
4. Don't blame the ex.

Rule 1: Assess His Finances

When your relationship becomes more serious, you will want to find out as much as possible about his financial situation. When you first start dating regularly, you should discuss divorce-related finances generally, such as whether he pays child support and maintenance, or if he has debt. This will help you gauge how strapped he is, so you can plan how you spend your time together. If he's broke, you will have to cook more and eat out less, for example. Then, once your relationship becomes more serious and you are thinking about a future together, full financial disclosure to one another is perfectly normal, and smart. This isn't about assessing his wealth—it's about knowing what you're getting into. You cannot plan your future if you don't know where you both stand financially.

You will want to know:

- How much he makes
- His debt (credit card, student loans, cars, etc.)
- His assets (savings, investments, property, businesses)
- How much he pays in child support and/or maintenance
- What his credit looks like

You will provide the same information. You should also ask to read his divorce agreement, which will not only detail how much he pays in child support and maintenance, but for how long he must pay. Once you assess all these factors, you will probably find that you can make the finances work, and that financials are rarely a deal-breaker. However, you may also find that you can't always afford the little luxuries, like eating out or frequent travel. The trick is to know all of these things *up front*, so they don't turn into the wolf down the road.

If, however, you see signs of trouble, such as credit problems or deep debt, you will want to avoid mingling finances with him. He needs to prove he can not only fix those problems on his own, but also show financial responsibility in the future. The good news is that most financial difficulties are surmountable—debts can be paid off, and maintenance and child support should eventually cease.

Rule 2: Don't Rescue Him

Some separated and divorced men face the occasional financial crisis, especially if they're in the middle of a divorce. During this time, you may find yourself tempted to help him. *Don't do it.* Don't give him money, loan him money, or merge finances in order to "share the burden."

There are a number of reasons that being his rescuer could prove to be a bad idea—for both of you:

He got himself into this. Thus, he can get himself out. His financial situation, no matter how pitiful, is the direct result of his behavior. Even if his ex put them into deep debt, he allowed it to happen instead of cutting her off. You should never have to pay for a man's mistakes. And you certainly shouldn't have to pay for his ex's mistakes! Let him crawl his way out of the mess—you will both feel better about it in the long run.

He will see you as his rescuer. As corny as it sounds, most men don't like to be rescued. He may accept money from you, but it might make him feel that he is inferior to you—and you don't want to worry about having to boost his ego to make up for it. Likewise, deep down, you may find that you resent having to clean up his mess.

You will probably regret it. It is the exception when a woman, in hindsight, is glad she gave money to a financially troubled man. This is a very easy way to wind up in a Low Output situation—giving or loaning money to a man represents a serious form of Input, with little Output. If your relationship fails, you will have nothing whatsoever to show for your "investment."

These rules apply whether he is moving out of his marital home, struggling through a divorce, or already divorced. They also apply when you move in together. When you share a home, to some extent you must share the financial burdens. But generally speaking, let him pay his obligations to his past life, and you will figure out a way to split the bills according to how much each of you has left after he pays his obligations. However, don't merge your finances, as it can complicate things with his child support or maintenance obligations. If you get married, you can still protect your assets. The laws vary from state to state—do your research, talk to a lawyer, and consider a prenuptial agreement.

Rule 3: Keep Your Job

If you have visions of quitting work when you get serious with or marry a divorced man, think again. Even if he could afford to support you, which may be difficult for a divorced man with financial obligations, quitting work can have considerable ramifications for you and for your relationship. Here are reasons it may be a good idea for you to keep your job.

You may have limited resources. The divorced man, especially the divorced man with children, often has significant financial obligations above and beyond those of everyday life. If you don't work, you may have to take a considerable cut in your lifestyle. Even a small income can bring in enough money to make a difference in lifestyle.

You become another one of his dependents. If he pays child support and maintenance to his ex, you may feel more like another dependent rather than his partner. Keeping your job takes pressure off him and helps him see you as an equal.

Giving up your job means giving up power. No matter how much each partner may contribute to the running of a household, the one who brings home the money holds the most power. If you don't have a job, you will have to ask for spending money, or you may resent him if he spends money on something you disagree with. If you keep your job, you have power because you contribute hard cash to the partnership.

You may become resentful. If he must pay his ex a large sum of money each month, having no job may contribute to your feeling resentful that you must "compete" for his money. This brings the phrase "economic polygamy" to a new level. Remember, having control over money is just as important as having money. Keeping your job means you have control over the money you bring to the union and you don't have to share it with his ex or anyone else.

Obviously, down the road, if you and he have a child together, you may need to stop working for a while. But as a rule, bringing in your own income maintains balance when you have a relationship with a divorced man.

Rule 4: Don't Blame the Ex

If his ex has anything to do with his financial difficulties, you may blame her and feel negatively toward her. Perhaps she was the one who overspent during their marriage, or didn't pay her bills during the divorce (harming his credit), or receives a large sum of money from him every month but has never gotten a job. Who can blame you? Who wants to be negatively impacted by someone else's financial irresponsibility? However, before you become too angry with her, here are some important things to remember.

He's paying for the past. If he pays his ex maintenance, it's probably because she cared for the children or supported him in some way that allowed him to advance in his job or career. He chose that path and now he must pay for it.

He may have agreed to it. Many men willingly pay the ex a lot of money because they don't want to look selfish or mean, or because they want to keep her from starting trouble. This is especially true if he left her. Thus, you can hardly blame her for accepting the cash.

He didn't stand up to her. It's hard to respect a woman who overspent marital funds on clothing or other luxuries, or who didn't pay her bills, creating financial troubles for the both of them. However, why didn't he stand up to his wife and demand that she control her spending or take care of her bills?

She's ultimately responsible for herself. If his ex refuses to work, continues to demand more money from him, or created financial problems that are affecting you, that will be frustrating for you. But there will come a time when the money runs out and she must face supporting herself, which won't be easy for her.

However, the most important reason for not blaming the ex has nothing to do with whose fault it is; blaming her gives away your power to something you have no control over, which only makes you resentful. The truth is, the only power you have in this type of situation is over yourself. That is why you should educate yourself about the divorced man's financials, and then formulate a plan for your future. Make sure you take care of yourself first, and let him handle his own problems.

The Last Word

Overall, you can work through most money issues you encounter when you have a relationship with a separated or divorced man. The trick is for you to get informed, and be prepared. However, you need to be honest with yourself: if you dislike where he is financially, it's better to slow things down or to cut your losses now than to swallow your discomfort, stick around, and then complain about it later. Every woman has different needs when it comes to money—find out what yours are, and stick to them.

FIFTEEN

Beyond Dating

By now, you probably have a pretty good idea about what's involved in *dating* separated and divorced men. However, the issues you face with these men change when your relationship becomes more serious—that is, when you move in together, get married, and/or have children. Marriage to divorced men, forming stepfamilies, and becoming a stepmother are complicated topics, and go beyond the scope of this book. There are many books that can give you a detailed picture of how your life will change when you take on marriage to a divorced man. However, because dating a divorced man sometimes leads to marriage and blending families, we will touch upon the very basics of marrying a divorced man—and all that comes with it.

The remainder of this book will do two things:

1. It will help you evaluate whether a future with a divorced man is right for you.
2. It will give you a preview of some of the main problems women face when marrying divorced men.

Is a Future with a Divorced Man Right for You?

So you've dated and gotten involved with a separated or divorced man. Now things are getting serious and you've begun talking about the future—moving in together or getting married. However, marrying a divorced man is very different from dating one, and it will be important for you to make sure that a future with him is right for you. Here are three things you must ask yourself before committing to a future with a divorced man:

1. Are there any red flags?
2. Do you have similar values?
3. Are you getting your needs met?

Question 1: Are There Any Red Flags?

A red flag is a warning. It can be a serious problem, something that makes you uncomfortable or just doesn't feel "right," or a sign of future problems. A red flag does not have to mean that the deal is off, but it does mean that you *must* solve it before you move in with or marry this man. Remember, any problems that occur during dating will only get worse with marriage. Thus, you should contemplate everything that bothers you about your relationship or concerns you about the future, and talk with friends or a therapist about it. Although a comprehensive list of possible red flags is beyond the scope of this book, here are ten red flags that are specific to divorced men. You should consider these very seriously before moving in with and especially before marrying a divorced man.

TEN RED FLAGS TO LOOK FOR

Red Flag #1: He is still grieving his marriage. The signs of grief span a broad spectrum, and I cover these signs in Chapter 3. You deserve a man who is totally ready to be with you.

Red Flag #2: He doesn't want marriage or kids. This is okay *only* if you feel 100 percent the same. You should never compromise on your desires for marriage or children.

Red Flag #3: He hasn't been divorced a year yet. A recent divorce usually means a much greater likelihood of many of the problems discussed in this book, including unresolved grief in kids, the ex, and family. Take your time.

Red Flag #4: He tells you his kids will always come first. I discuss this complicated issue in Chapter 10, and in the next chapter in "Common Reasons Stepfamilies Struggle." You should never accept second place in marriage.

Red Flag #5: He hasn't learned from his mistakes. See Chapter 6 for the signs. A man who hasn't learned from his mistakes will only make them again with you.

Red Flag #6: He has poor boundaries with his ex. Perhaps he's always helping her out, or he lets her treat you poorly. See the signs in Chapter 8. Poor boundaries with the ex will only make you unhappy and take a toll on your relationship.

Red Flag #7: His kids don't like you, or vice versa. By now, any initial discomfort with his kids should be gone. A family should be based on mutual caring and respect, not merely tolerance.

Red Flag #8: He's not a good father. Although no father is perfect, avoid Guilty, Disneyland, and Under-involved Dads. These dads will make your life with him much more difficult. See Chapter 10.

Red Flag #9: He has poor boundaries with his family or friends. If he doesn't handle his family or friends appropriately, or lets them disrespect you, you will not be happy with him. See Chapter 12.

Red Flag #10: He has serious debts or bad credit from his marriage. Debts and credit problems can be signs of financial irresponsibility, and will have a significant impact on your future with him. See Chapter 14.

This isn't an exhaustive list—you should think of any and all red flags about the way he treats you, how you feel about him, and even your sex life. **Ultimately, do not move in with and certainly don't marry or reproduce with him until you eradicate all red flags.**

Question 2: Do You Have Similar Values?

Values are basic, fundamental beliefs that influence how you live your life, how you behave in a relationship, and how you raise your children. To say that similar values are important for a successful marriage would be a huge understatement. When moving in with or marrying a divorced man, especially one with children, values come into play in several areas, including:

- How the two of you handle his children, ex-spouse, family, and friends
- How you handle your finances together
- How you deal with conflict
- How you divide household duties
- Your role in dealing with his children
- Your role and priority in his life

You and he must have similar values in these areas, or no matter how smooth your dating goes, your living together or marriage will be rocky.

> ҈ Linda was engaged to marry Tom, a divorced man with two children. Things had been looking pretty good, as Tom loved Linda, Tom's kids liked Linda, and Tom's ex was a Polite/Absent Ex. However, after spending more time together with Tom's kids, Linda began to find things she didn't like. The kids spent most of their time watching television, whereas Linda felt that kids should be doing more active or useful things. Tom let his kids eat whatever they wanted, whereas Linda felt that he should teach them healthy eating habits. Most importantly, Linda was the last person considered when decisions were made about vacations and how free time was spent together. Ultimately, Linda broke off her engagement to Tom due to their value differences.

Television watching and eating habits may seem like small things, but they are indicative of important value systems—Tom was a laissez-faire father who felt that the kids would grow up fine without sweating the small stuff, and Linda was more authoritative and felt that children need more structure and guidance to grow up to be well-rounded adults. Further,

Tom felt that their free time should revolve around the kids and their desires, whereas Linda felt she deserved more say.

You and your partner should discuss your values ahead of time. However, the best way to determine someone's values is to observe their everyday behavior, as Linda did with Tom. Thus, make sure you pay attention to small, everyday things as well as big things. Even if you disagree initially, you may be able to come to agreement on how to handle these issues.

Question 3: Are You Getting Your Needs Met?

A divorced man, and any accompanying baggage he has, can be a lot for one woman to take on. Fortunately, as long as the red flags are tied up and put away, most baggage isn't the end of the world as long as you are prepared for it. However, even in a red-flag-free environment, you need to make triple sure you are getting your needs met in your relationship before you marry or reproduce with him. Sometimes living together before marrying may be required in order to really know if your relationship will meet your needs. However, whether or not to live together before marriage is a personal choice that you and he must make together. In general, when evaluating whether you are getting your needs met, you should think about the following points.

Input Versus Output

This is a concept introduced in Chapter 1 and touched upon throughout the book. When you are thinking about a future with a divorced man, you must examine how much you put into your relationship (Input) versus how much you get out of your relationship (Output).

To put it simply, your Output must be greater than your Input; otherwise, you will be miserable. But how do you know if your Output is high enough? Examine your level of happiness in your relationship, and in your life. Are you happy in your relationship most of the time? Or are you dealing with conflicts and problems on a regular basis? Are you getting your needs met? Talk to your friends and family: since you've been involved with this man, do you seem happier to them, or more stressed out? The happier you are, the greater your Output. Too much Input and too little Output creates a Low Output situation, which is the root of unhappiness in these relationships. As I mentioned in Chapter 1, "rescue" relationships are ideal for creating a Low Output situation. In a rescue relationship, a woman steps into a baggage-laden relationship with a divorced man and winds up trying to fix the mess. Here is an example:

5 Haley met divorced man Ron at a work-related conference. Ron had full custody of two teenaged boys, who visited their mother from time to time. The boys liked Haley, and eventually she and Ron planned on getting married. However, the boys' mother was not involved enough in their lives, leaving Haley to feel responsible for them. Ron, although a good father, did not provide them with all the guidance he could have. Finally, Ron paid his ex a sizeable sum of money each month, leaving him with little money. As the wedding approached, Haley began to feel pressured, realizing that a lot of Ron's child and financial burdens would be heaped upon her when they married. She would have to be the rescuer, by trying to be both the mother the boys didn't have and the financial provider. Haley broke off their engagement.

Fortunately, Haley could see that marrying Ron would put her in a Low Output situation. She had begun to feel her Output dwindling during her engagement to Ron, and examined her situation carefully. Leaving Ron was not an easy decision for Haley, but she knew it was the best choice in the long run.

Input versus Output applies to all relationships, not just relationships with divorced men. However, because divorced men can come with difficulties, the risk for getting into a Low Output situation is greater. Thus, take your time and pay close attention to how you feel. If you feel happy and content, you are probably getting enough Output relative to your Input. But if you feel unhappy, stressed, or as if you're always solving one problem after the next, beware—you may be in a Low Output situation.

Loving Him Is Required, but It Isn't Enough

We all want to believe that love conquers all. However, while love can go a long way in enriching our lives, love by itself will not make us happy. Thus, loving the divorced man is required, but it isn't enough to make the relationship succeed. When evaluating whether to marry a divorced man, don't just ask yourself, "Do I love him?" or "Do I want to be with him?" Also ask yourself, "Do I feel happy, or stressed out?" and "Is the life I have with this divorced man, and all he comes with, consistent with who I am?" No matter how much you love him, love won't be enough if the situation doesn't meet your needs, leaves you in a Low Output situation, or is basically not right for you.

If you take Haley and Ron's example, there is no question that Haley loved Ron. However, she found that love wasn't enough—the relationship wasn't the right one for her. Your relationship doesn't have to be problem-free—no relationship is without its problems. But in addition to love, you should feel happy in the relationship the vast majority of the time.

Don't Settle

At some point, you may feel uncomfortable with your relationship. You may experience frustration with the relationship, or doubts over whether you belong with him. And at this point, some dating "expert," your mother, or a well-meaning friend may tell you the most pernicious thing that a woman can ever say to another woman: **"No man is perfect."**

They will tell you that all men, divorced or not, have issues, whether it's relationship baggage, commitment-phobia, or other imperfections. They will tell you that by leaving the set of problems you get with your divorced man, you will only encounter a new set of problems with someone else. The pernicious aspect of this statement isn't its falseness—it's true, no man is perfect. The real problem is the message *behind* the message: that you should tolerate things you aren't comfortable with in your relationship. Never, ever fall for this philosophy, for a few reasons:

First, divorced men appeal to many women because these men's previous marriages prove that they can commit. Assuming they're willing to commit again, that's a good thing. But although commitment is required for a successful relationship, it is not enough by itself. Once a commitment-hungry woman gets her commitment need met, she then realizes she has a variety of other needs that she never recognized because they were overshadowed by the commitment issue. In other words, choosing a man simply because he's willing to commit is settling.

Second, every woman has different needs. One woman may cringe at the idea of being a stepmother, whereas another would find it fulfilling. One woman may hate that he's friends with his ex, whereas another wouldn't mind at all. The goal is not to find a perfect man, because no man is perfect; it's to find the perfect man *for you*. And if you're having doubts, you should explore them completely before making any permanent commitments. The bottom line? **Never settle for less than what you need. It will only lead to unhappiness.**

All that said, marrying a divorced man, no matter how baggage-laden, is not necessarily settling. Settling is accepting less than what you really want and need from a relationship, and only you know what you really want or need. Only you know what's best for you. Thus, if you are happy with your divorced man, no matter what his situation, then go for it.

SIXTEEN

Three Things to Consider When Moving In with or Marrying a Man with Children

Think about the last time you were waiting to begin a new challenge in your life—perhaps when you were about to start your freshman year of college, or were preparing to run your first marathon, or were about to have your first child. No matter how much you prepared for that event, the event itself was probably more challenging than you expected. However, being prepared almost certainly helped you a lot. The studying you did for college, the training you underwent for the marathon, and the reading you did about childbirth—the more you knew about what to expect, the less surprised you were by the challenges and struggles you faced. That's why we have books, classes, friends, training programs, and other ways to inform us.

Well, becoming a member of a stepfamily is one of those challenges—it's difficult to know what it will be like until you actually do it. And the more information you have, the more prepared you will be for any difficulties that might come up.

If you are thinking about moving in with or marrying a divorced man with children, you should read all you can about the subject. You will find a lot of "scary" stories, but will find some inspiring ones as well. As you read, you will find that many of these books stress three important things for you to consider when you are blending families:

1. Common reasons stepfamilies struggle
2. Things stepmoms struggle with
3. When you want a child of your own

Point #1: Common Reasons Stepfamilies Struggle

Why is the divorce rate for second marriages higher than for first marriages? And why do so many stepfamilies struggle? There can be many reasons, but research has shown that most stepfamily problems stem from the following things:

- Poor boundaries with children, the ex, or family
- Unrealistic expectations
- Not putting the marriage first
- Role confusion
- Incompatibility regarding childrearing and house rules
- Failure to learn from the first marriage
- An unwillingness to get help

Poor Boundaries with Children, the Ex, or Family

Countless women who have become stepmothers have encountered poorly behaved children, children sleeping in the marital bed, intrusive or rude exes, and disrespectful or intrusive in-laws. These women are put through so much pain and difficulty because their husbands haven't learned the importance of boundaries. In addition, new stepmothers often have their own boundary problems as well, and may overstep their role by trying to overparent stepchildren, deal with the ex, or fix everyone's problems. Thus, establishing good boundaries is good for everyone, and a good book and/ or therapist can help with boundary issues.

Unrealistic Expectations

Because most people who create a stepfamily have never been in one before, they often form unrealistic expectations. Typically, these expectations are based on how "original" families look, or on whatever norms they grew up with. One way a stepmother develops unrealistic expectations is when she expects to bond with her husband's children as if she were their mother. This usually results in disappointment, as the children already have a mother and she's known them a lot longer. Here are a few guidelines:

- Don't expect to love them like they're your own children. This does not mean you can't love them—it means it will be a different type of love.
- Don't expect them to love you like they love their parents. Again, this doesn't mean they can't love you—it will just be a different type of love.
- Don't try to parent them like you're their mother. You can be an authority and maintain rules, but let their natural parents handle raising and disciplining them.

Not Putting the Marriage First

In Chapter 10, I discussed that while *dating* a divorced man, your importance in his life, and in his heart, will rise to that of his children as your relationship becomes more committed. However, once your commitment becomes long-term, your importance in his life will change again—you should be first in his life. Many people, in their quest to be good parents or providers, forget that in successful marriages *the marital relationship comes first*. This means making time to be together without the children, keeping the lines of communication open, and keeping the romance alive. However, it also means showing children that while they are dearly loved, they do not come before their parent's spouse, whether it's their mother or their stepmother. This is what I mean when I say that once you make a long-term commitment with a divorced man, his children should not come first. The reasoning behind this is that a solid marriage provides a solid foundation to raise children, and makes children feel more secure. The more secure children feel, the less likely they are to act out.

Some people don't understand this idea—they want to be good parents and they lose sight of not only their role, but also their children's roles. Thus, they dote on their children and treat them like they are equal to, or more important than, their spouse. However, while children are equal to a spouse in terms of love, they are not equal to the spouse in terms of their role in the family. When people have children, it is their job to raise and care for those children until they become adults. As the children develop, they become less and less dependent on the parent, until ultimately they strike out on their own. In other words, parents raise children to go out and have their own lives. However, when two people get married, they are committing to be the most important person in each other's lives—they are always equals, and partners for life. The role they play in each other's lives remains the same. Thus, when a man marries or otherwise forms a long-term partnership with a woman, she takes first place in his life.

This does not mean that a man's children are less important than his wife, or that he loves his children less. It does
not mean that the couple ignores the children's needs. It
means that in healthy families, the marriage is the foundation of the family, and therefore comes first. Here are some
ways a long-term partner comes first:

- He demands that his children treat his partner with
  respect, period.
- The couple makes all important family-based decisions
  together, and he consults his wife before asking the children's opinion. This shows the children that his wife is an
  authority in the house, on par with Dad.
- The couple decides on all household rules together.
- Children have input into household issues, but no final
  decision-making power.
- He turns to his spouse for love and support, not his
  children.
- When conflicts occur, he stands by his partner and backs
  her up.
- The children don't enter the marital bedroom without
  asking first, or touch or borrow their stepmother's belongings without asking first.

A related question is "Don't the children's needs come
first?" The answer is simple: nobody's needs "come first."
In a family, we don't tell one family member that his or
her needs matter more than the needs of the others. However, as discussed in Chapter 10, there are times when the
everyday demands of parenting require that a child's needs
will take precedent over an adult's, especially when children are young. This includes getting children to school and
to activities, caring for them when they're sick, and all the
other realities of parenting dependent children. Most parents

already know what's required of them as parents—but they don't always know what's required of them as spouses.

Role Confusion

This is one of the most difficult aspects of creating a stepfamily. Most people, naturally, approach their stepfamily role as they would approach their role in an "original" family—it's the only role they know. However, this isn't always the best way. Even in this day and age, women tend to take on a caretaking role in families; often, Dad is the breadwinner and Mom is home with the kids. We've all seen exceptions to this rule, but overall, this is still the most common setup. Why is this important when getting involved with a divorced man with children? Because these familiar roles don't always work well in stepfamilies. You will often see women take on the "mom" role in the new family: clean house and provide meals, take the kids to school, take care of them during the day while Dad is at work. They often deal with the ex regarding pickup times, or regulate how much the children watch TV. Some women wind up mothering the children while Dad works a lot or goes on business trips. While pretty standard for many moms, this is inappropriate for a stepmom, as she is still new in the children's lives, and she is not their mother. It puts too much pressure on her, takes too much responsibility off the father, and can engender resentment in the children. If both the stepmom and kids are happy with this arrangement, then it's fine. Otherwise, everybody has to shift roles—Dad must be more of a "mother" and the stepmom must be less of one in some ways. However, the stepmom is still an authority.

Figuring out the family roles takes time and patience. This is where preparation, reading, and therapy can be very useful. You should discuss with your partner the role you will take in the new family, and how you will handle his children, your children (if you have them), and rules and discipline. Here are pointers that can help avoid future problems:

- Your primary role is to be your partner's partner, not the kids' parent. His children already have two parents, and no matter what you think of their parenting skills, it's their job to raise the kids, not yours. Realizing this will relieve some of the pressure you may feel.
- While it's okay to help your partner out with caring for the children, don't become their cook, maid, or chauffeur. This role comes with being a primary parent and if you do too much of this, you will begin to feel resentful or unappreciated.
- Let your partner discipline his children. You and your partner can create and enforce the house rules, but leave the main discipline to Dad, especially during the first few years together.
- Don't force your values on his kids—for example, don't tell them how to dress or what to believe. While you should partner up with a man who shares your value systems, it is ultimately between him and their mother to decide how the children are raised.
- Let time tell what specific role you will play in his children's lives. You may be Dad's wife, whom they are respectful to, or a mother figure whom they look up to. It all depends on the situation, what the children are comfortable with, and what you are comfortable with.
- Discuss with your partner what his kids will call you. In most situations, they will call you by your name, but a nickname or an occasional "Mom" isn't that unusual. **Never ask a stepchild to call you Mom, no matter what.** However, if they want to call you Mom, let them do so if you and their father are comfortable with it.

Incompatibility Regarding Childrearing and House Rules

As discussed in Question 2 in the previous chapter, similar values are key to making any marriage work. In stepfamilies, they are especially important; because the biological parent and stepparent did not create their family "from scratch," they may have very different notions as to how the children should behave and what rules should be followed. Plus, there is a third party, the kids' mother, who may have rules of her own. If you and your partner do not agree on how to handle the children and the house rules, the results will be disastrous: you will fight, and the children will sense your discord and take advantage of it, which will only lead to more conflict. Thus, one way or another, you and he must come to an agreement on how to handle childrearing and house rules.

Failure to Learn from the First Marriage

As mentioned in Chapter 6, some men do not learn why their first marriages failed, and go on to make the same mistakes in the next marriage. It's important that he understand what went wrong in the first marriage, what he did to contribute to it, and what he should do better next time.

In addition, research has shown that men, more than women, achieve considerable health benefits from being married. Moreover, divorced men remarry more quickly than women do, on average. One reason a divorced man, especially a divorced man with children, may be quick to remarry is because he is somewhat "lost" without the things a woman provides a family. This type of man often relies too much on a woman to do what he considers "women's work," including caring for his children. This traditional division of labor may work in original marriages, but it doesn't work at all in stepfamilies because the stepmother cannot fulfill the same mother role with the children. There is nothing wrong with wanting a woman in his life, but the divorced man needs to realize that his days of letting his partner do the "women's work" are over.

An Unwillingness to Get Help

Stepfamilies face many challenges, many of which are unfamiliar to the average person. Not too long ago, it wasn't uncommon for a stepfamily to be the only stepfamily on the block, or the only stepfamily in their circle or friends—thus, when things went wrong, they had no one to talk to. But today, with stepfamilies becoming the norm in our society, there are more and more resources to help, including the following:

- Stepfamily Web sites and organizations such as the Stepfamily Association of America (*www.saafamilies.org*) and the Stepfamily Foundation (*www.stepfamily.org*)
- Books on stepparenting and stepfamilies
- Therapists who understand stepfamily dynamics

It's important to get help when times get tough, especially from resources that understand the unique challenges that come with stepfamilies.

Point #2: Things Stepmoms Struggle With

Stepparenting can be a difficult job. If you talk with enough stepmoms about the difficulties of stepparenting, you will often hear many of the same complaints from them. Here are some of the more common ones.

"No One Appreciates All I Do."

Everyone knows that mothering is a tough job—but women do it because of the intrinsic reward that comes from raising their own children. However, taking on the traditional mother role in a stepfamily means taking on that tough job without the same kind of reward, and without the final say in deciding how the children are raised. If she cooks, cleans, and shuttles the kids around, and then they don't love her (or even like her), all that hard work is going to seem pretty pointless very quickly. This is compounded when his ex-wife doesn't like her or appreciate her caring for the children.

"My Husband Doesn't Do Enough."

Too often, stepmothers wind up taking care of the logistics of running a household, including cooking, cleaning, and dealing with the day-to-day aspects of children. They often wind up dealing with the children's mother and even her family. Eventually, conflicts ensue. At that point, her partner may step back and let her take the heat, which only puts more pressure on her. Moreover, some fathers don't know how to parent their children effectively, creating chaos in the household and putting more pressure on his partner to create order.

"My Stepchildren or In-Laws Are Disrespectful to Me."

This is perhaps the most common complaint stepmothers have, and the one that can be the most hurtful. A woman should *never* have to tolerate disrespectful or rude behavior from her partner's children, ex-wife, parents, or anybody else. This happens when a man does not know how to manage the people in his life. He needs to step in, establish rules and boundaries, and set the example for everybody else by supporting his partner.

"I Never Come First."

You've heard the saying "The squeaky wheel gets the oil." Well, children, ex-wives, and family can get pretty squeaky at times, and he may seek to quiet the noise, forgetting what (and who) is most important. Just dealing with children's needs, problems, and conflicts can be especially time-consuming; some of this goes with the territory when he has children, but sometimes parents forget their priorities and focus too much on the children.

Fortunately, these problems are fixable when both partners are willing to work together to solve them. Anything you and your partner can do ahead of time to prevent some of these problems will only make things easier down the road.

Point #3: When You Want a Child of Your Own

If you desire children of your own, be sure to choose a partner who is completely willing to have children with you. The last thing you want is to marry a man who isn't sure he wants more children, and then decides he has enough on his plate with his own children. In addition, you need to consider whether he is just *willing* to have more kids or truly *interested* in having more kids. Raising a child is a huge responsibility, and if he isn't 100 percent up for the task, you might have to be prepared to take on many of the child-care responsibilities.

If you read books or talk with people about having a child with a divorced man, especially a divorced man with children, be prepared for some greatly differing opinions on what to expect. Based on other women's experiences, here are some pros and cons of having a baby with a man who already has children.

The Pros

Many women say that having a baby put them on equal footing in the stepfamily. When you marry a man with children, to some extent you are the "outsider" because you don't share the blood bonds or, often, the long-term history that he shares with his children and his ex. Thus, having a child with him "cements" your bond to the family. Plus, since extended families often focus on children, having a child tends to garner more attention and priority from them than you would get otherwise. After all, your baby will share his family's genes, and blood bonds are powerful. However, it isn't a good idea to bring a child into the world just to get equal footing in your family—make sure you're ready to be a biological parent.

The Cons

On the other hand, some women complain that they have to compete with his other children for attention and resources, that he may feel guilty for having less time and money for his first set of children, or that he will resent having to raise and support yet another child. These women wind up taking on many of the child-care responsibilities alone.

Prevent the "Cons" by making sure he is ready and willing to have a child with you.

Are You Cut Out for Stepfamily Life?

As you've probably gathered from reading this chapter, step-families have unique challenges of their own. Although there are no specific traits that guarantee stepfamily success, here are eleven traits that will make stepfamily life easier for you:

1. You grew up in a stepfamily, and thus have more realistic expectations.
2. You aren't especially old-fashioned, and don't mind a "blended" family.
3. You have a career and don't want to be a homemaker.
4. You aren't possessive and don't get jealous easily.
5. You love children.
6. You are maternal, and enjoy caring for children.
7. You are easygoing about house rules.
8. You don't mind not always being in charge.
9. You have a high tolerance for stress.
10. You have a job, friends, and hobbies of your own.
11. You are comfortable with who you are.

However, even if you don't have many of these traits, this doesn't mean you can't marry a divorced man with children. It means you may have more challenges to face. Stepfamilies require a certain amount of flexibility, open-mindedness, and patience—but with the right amount of planning and effort, you can have a happy, successful stepfamily.

CONCLUSION

The Final Word

Throughout this book, you have learned many challenges you could face when you date a separated or divorced man. You have also been armed with guidance for anticipating and handling those challenges. However, while this book is intended to provide you a road map for navigating the unfamiliar territory of separated and divorced men, the problems presented are not intended to scare you away from these men, or to make these men sound like bad people. Separated and divorced men aren't bad at all—but they can have their share of challenges, and the purpose of this book is to tell you what those are. If you were planning to run a marathon, wouldn't you want to know the biggest challenges to completing a marathon successfully? Wouldn't you want a list of worst-case scenarios, and how to prevent them? Ultimately, my goal is a simple one: whether you date a separated or divorced man for one evening, three months, or three years, or if you marry him, I want you to have a happy, successful relationship with him, where you get your needs met. I wish you the best of luck!

Index

men blaming, 79
men living in past and, 74–77
with new partners, 98
nonessential contact with, 75–76
not over him, 99–101
as permanent part of his life, 3,
103–4
Polite or Absent, 88, 96, 98,
103, 111, 113
problems with, 99–109
sharing him with, during
divorce, 56–57
similar to you, 79
who initiated divorce, 98
Ex-wives, dealing with, 110–23
being polite, 110–13
establishing boundaries,
116–18
if divorce not final, 115–16
minimizing her involvement,
113–14
protecting yourself, 118–21

Family and friends (his), 151–63
accepting only respect from,
170–72
assessing, 166–68
assessing relationship based on,
172–73
disapproving of your
relationship, 51, 52
displaying pictures of ex, 155,
169
disregarding you, 158–60
divided loyalties of, 160–61
divorce impacting, 152–53
establishing boundaries with,
168–70
giving them time, 164–66
grief affecting behavior, 153–54
him confronting, 168–70
him wimping out around,
161–63
holding on to past, 154–57
inviting ex to functions, 157
marriage creating bonds with,
152
not inviting you, 158
problems with, 154–63

putting you in middle, 169
questions to ask, 166–67
referring to ex as his wife,
156–57
rudeness to you, 159, 168–69
rules for dealing with, 164–73
talking about ex, 155–56, 169
Family and friends (yours)
being difficult, 171–72
keeping in your life, 62–64
Finances. See Money
Future beyond dating, 194–203.
See also Remarriage;
Stepfamilies
comparing values, 197–99
Input vs. Output and, 199–201
needs fulfillment and, 199–203
not settling, 202–3
red-flag cautions, 195–97

Grieving men, 9
in process of divorce, 46–48
separated, 31–34
signs of, 32–33
soon-to-be-separated, 22–23
time since divorce and, 12–13
Guilt (his), xiii
guilty dads, 134–35, 137, 197
having child with him and,
215
not being over marriage and,
22–23, 33, 47–48, 103–4
overindulgence and, 185–87
using you to absolve, 21–22

Infidelity, 13
Input vs. Output, 15–17, 61, 68–
69, 89, 148, 150, 189, 199–201

Job, keeping, 190–91

Kids. See Children

Losses, feelings of, 72–73

Maintenance (alimony), 178–83
assessing finances and, 187–88
assessing his baggage and, 88
described, 178–79

About the Author

CHRISTIE HARTMAN, PH.D., received her M.A. in clinical psychology in 2001 and is currently employed at the University of Colorado. She has taught college-level psychology and presented original research at national conferences. She also has considerable personal experience with dating separated and divorced men and has conducted extensive research on dating, divorce, and stepfamilies. She lives in Denver, CO.